Kim Maya Sutton

How Contemporary Publishers Reach Out to Their Customers

Transition from B2B to B2C Marketing in the Publishing Industry

Diplomica Verlag GmbH

Sutton, Kim Maya: How Contemporary Publishers Reach Out to Their Customers:
Transition from B2B to B2C Marketing in the Publishing Industry, Hamburg,
Diplomica Verlag GmbH 2013

Buch-ISBN: 978-3-8428-6100-8
PDF-eBook-ISBN: 978-3-8428-1100-3
Druck/Herstellung: Diplomica® Verlag GmbH, Hamburg, 2013
Covermotiv: © Kim Maya Sutton

Bibliografische Information der Deutschen Nationalbibliothek:
Die Deutsche Nationalbibliothek verzeichnet diese Publikation in der Deutschen
Nationalbibliografie; detaillierte bibliografische Daten sind im Internet über
http://dnb.d-nb.de abrufbar.

Das Werk einschließlich aller seiner Teile ist urheberrechtlich geschützt. Jede Verwertung
außerhalb der Grenzen des Urheberrechtsgesetzes ist ohne Zustimmung des Verlages
unzulässig und strafbar. Dies gilt insbesondere für Vervielfältigungen, Übersetzungen,
Mikroverfilmungen und die Einspeicherung und Bearbeitung in elektronischen Systemen.

Die Wiedergabe von Gebrauchsnamen, Handelsnamen, Warenbezeichnungen usw. in
diesem Werk berechtigt auch ohne besondere Kennzeichnung nicht zu der Annahme,
dass solche Namen im Sinne der Warenzeichen- und Markenschutz-Gesetzgebung als frei
zu betrachten wären und daher von jedermann benutzt werden dürften.

Die Informationen in diesem Werk wurden mit Sorgfalt erarbeitet. Dennoch können
Fehler nicht vollständig ausgeschlossen werden und die Diplomica Verlag GmbH, die
Autoren oder Übersetzer übernehmen keine juristische Verantwortung oder irgendeine
Haftung für evtl. verbliebene fehlerhafte Angaben und deren Folgen.

Alle Rechte vorbehalten

© Diplomica Verlag GmbH
Hermannstal 119k, 22119 Hamburg
http://www.diplomica-verlag.de, Hamburg 2013
Printed in Germany

Acknowledgements

I would like to thank my supervisors Mal Peachey and Dr. Samantha Rayner for their numerous hours of support, advice, and guidance, which contributed to the quality of this research and my own growth as a researcher.

My special thanks go to my family and my friends who have supported me throughout my Master studies. Your love, support, and distraction gave me strength. In particular: Mutti, without you, I would not have been able to pursue this Master course and you always believed in me; Will, without you, I could not have hung in there; Mozart, without you, I would be in a horrible shape both in body and spirit.

Glossary

B2B	Business-to-business
B2C	Business-to-consumer or business-to-customer
Blog	Shortened form of web log; can contain text, media, videos, images, links, and is usually interactive in that it allows readers to comment and send messages.
E-tailer	Retailer who sells electronically, e.g. via the Internet
Facebook	General social networking site with more than 650 million users
RSS	Resource Description Framework Site Summary: regular web feeds sent to subscribers of webpages
Tweet	News flash on Twitter limited to 140 characters
Twitter	Microblogging site with more than 175 million users
URL	Uniform Resource Locator: specification where resource is and how to retrieve it
YouTube	Video-sharing website

Abbreviations

et seq.	*et sequens* (and the following page)
et seqq.	*et sequentes* (and the following pages)
p.	page
pp.	pages
UK	United Kingdom
USA	United States of America

Table of Contents

1 Introduction 13
  1.1 Synopsis 13
  1.2 Background to Research 14
  1.3 Research Questions 15
  1.4 Methodology 15
    1.4.1 Research Undertaken 15
    1.4.2 Data Collection Requirements 16
    1.4.3 Limitations and Researcher's Background 16
  1.5 Outline of the Dissertation 17
  1.6 Contribution of Research and Conclusion 17

2 Marketing in the Publishing Industry 19
  2.1 Introduction 19
  2.2 Key Terms Defined 19
    2.2.1 Definition of Marketing 19
    2.2.2 Definition of Publisher 20
  2.3 Introduction to Marketing 20
  2.4 Publishers' Marketing 21
    2.4.1 Differentiation from Other Industries 21
    2.4.2 Types of Publishers' Marketing 22
    2.4.3 Marketing Expenditure and Target Audience 23
  2.5 Traditional B2C Marketing in the Publishing Industry 23
    2.5.1 Brand 23
    2.5.2 Book Design 24
    2.5.3 Media Attention 24
    2.5.4 Reading Initiatives and Prizes 24
    2.5.5 Viral Marketing 25
  2.6 B2C E-marketing in the Publishing Industry 25
    2.6.1 Introduction 25
    2.6.2 Online Consumers' Needs 26
    2.6.3 Publishers' Websites 26
    2.6.4 Social Media and Blogs 27
    2.6.5 Stages of Managing Social Technology 28
    2.6.6 Other Trends 28
      2.6.6.1 Gardners' Hive 28
      2.6.6.2 Involving Authors 29
      2.6.6.3 Other Online Networks 29
      2.6.6.4 Affinity Schemes 29
      2.6.6.5 E-books 30
      2.6.6.6 Odyl 30
  2.7 Conclusion 30

3 Conceptual Model 33
  3.1 Introduction 33
  3.2 Current Publishers' B2C Marketing 33
  3.3 Limitations of this Model 35
  3.4 Conclusion 35

4 Researched Publishers 37
4.1 Introduction 37
4.2 Overview of Publishers 38
4.3 In-Depth Case Profiles 38
4.3.1 Salt Publishing 39
4.3.1.1 Publisher Profile 39
4.3.1.2 Website 39
4.3.1.3 Social Media 39
4.3.1.4 Consumer Response 40
4.3.1.5 Frontlist E-marketing 40
4.3.1.6 Summary Salt Publishing 40
4.3.2 Nosy Crow 44
4.3.2.1 Publisher Profile 44
4.3.2.2 Website 44
4.3.2.3 Social Media 44
4.3.2.4 Consumer Response 45
4.3.2.5 Frontlist E-marketing 45
4.3.2.6 Summary Nosy Crow 45
4.3.3 PS Publishing 47
4.3.3.1 Publisher Profile 47
4.3.3.2 Website 47
4.3.3.3 Social Media 47
4.3.3.4 Consumer Response 48
4.3.3.5 Frontlist E-marketing 48
4.3.3.6 Summary PS Publishing 48
4.3.4 Gollancz 51
4.3.4.1 Publisher Profile 51
4.3.4.2 Website 51
4.3.4.3 Social Media 51
4.3.4.4 Consumer Response 52
4.3.4.5 Frontlist E-marketing 52
4.3.4.6 Summary Gollancz 52
4.3.5 Bloomsbury 54
4.3.5.1 Publisher Profile 54
4.3.5.2 Website 54
4.3.5.3 Social Media 55
4.3.5.4 Consumer Response 55
4.3.5.5 Frontlist E-marketing 56
4.3.5.6 Summary Bloomsbury 56
4.3.6 Portobello Books 60
4.3.6.1 Publisher Profile 60
4.3.6.2 Website 60
4.3.6.3 Social Media 61
4.3.6.4 Consumer Response 61
4.3.6.5 Frontlist E-marketing 61
4.3.6.6 Summary Portobello 61

  4.3.7 Canongate 63
    4.3.7.1 Company Profile 63
    4.3.7.2 Website 63
    4.3.7.3 Social Media 63
    4.3.7.4 Consumer Response 64
    4.3.7.5 Frontlist E-marketing 64
    4.3.7.6 Summary Canongate 64
  4.4 Cross-Case Summary 68
    4.4.1 Overview 68
    4.4.2 Website 69
    4.4.4 Social Media 70
    4.4.5 Consumer Response 71
    4.4.6 Frontlist E-marketing 71
  4.5 Conclusion 72
5 Discussion of the Findings 73
  5.1 Introduction 73
  5.2 Findings 73
    5.2.1 Overview 73
    5.2.2 Product-Driven Marketing 74
    5.2.3 Marketing Planning 74
    5.2.4 360-Degree Marketing 75
    5.2.5 Fast-paced Technology 75
    5.2.6 Viral Marketing 75
    5.2.7 Trendsetting 76
  5.3 Implications and Revision to the Model 77
  5.4 Conclusion 78
6 Conclusions and Recommendations for Further Research 79
  6.1 Introduction 79
  6.2 Contribution to Knowledge and Recommendations 79
    6.2.1 How can publishers transition from B2B to B2C marketing (Q1)? 79
    6.2.2 How can publishers make use of social media (Q2)? 80
    6.2.3 How can publishers set up their websites to interest more consumers (Q3)? 80
    6.2.4 What can publishers learn from other companies' transition to a
       B2C marketing approach (Q4)? 80
  6.3 Limitations 81
  6.4 Implications for Further Research 81
  6.5 Conclusion 81

List of Figures

Figure 2.1 Marketing Types and How They Relate 20
Figure 3.1 Publishers' B2C Activities 34
Figure 4.1 Salt Main Webpage 41
Figure 4.2 Salt Navigation Bar 41
Figure 4.3 Salt Blog Categories and Recent Posts 41
Figure 4.4 Salt Social Media Links 41
Figure 4.5 Salt on Twitter 41
Figure 4.6 Salt on Facebook 42
Figure 4.7 Salt News 43
Figure 4.8 Salt on YouTube 43
Figure 4.9 Recommendation to Salt 43
Figure 4.10 Nosy Crow Links to Frontlist Book 46
Figure 4.11 Nosy Crow Contact Us 46
Figure 4.12 Nosy Crow Main Webpage 46
Figure 4.13 Nosy Crow Follow Us Invitations 46
Figure 4.14 PS Main Webpage 49
Figure 4.15 PS Tagged on YouTube 50
Figure 4.16 PS Book Review 50
Figure 4.17 PS Links 50
Figure 4.18 PS Social Networking Links 50
Figure 4.19 Gollancz Main Webpage 53
Figure 4.20 Gollancz Dark Fantasy Social Media 53
Figure 4.21 Gollancz Facebook Conversation One 53
Figure 4.22 Gollancz Facebook Conversation Two 53
Figure 4.23 Gollancz Facebook Conversation Three 53
Figure 4.24 Bloomsbury Main Webpage 57
Figure 4.25 Bloomsbury Additional Information 58
Figure 4.26 Bloomsbury Children's Books 58
Figure 4.27 Bloomsbury Harry Potter 58
Figure 4.28 Bloomsbury Social Media Links 58
Figure 4.29 Bloomsbury Sharing on Social Media 58
Figure 4.30 Bloomsbury Contact Us 59
Figure 4.31 Bloomsbury Frontlist Title 59
Figure 4.32 Portobello Books Main Webpage 62
Figure 4.33 Working With Portobello 62
Figure 4.34 Old Canongate Main Page 65
Figure 4.35 New Main Webpage Canongate 66
Figure 4.36 Canongate Reader Account 66
Figure 4.37 Canongate Link to Community 66
Figure 4.38 Canongate Social Media Invitation 67
Figure 4.39 Canongate Social Media Sharing 67
Figure 5.1 Publishers' B2C Activities (Adjusted Model) 77

List of Tables
Table 1.1 Dissertation Outline 17
Table 2.1 Publishers' Marketing Efforts.. 22
Table 2.2 Bernoff's Stages of Managing Social Technology 28
Table 4.1 Case Profiles.. 38
Table 4.2 Publishers' B2C Efforts 68
Table 4.3 Statistics for Publishers on Social Networking Sites 70
Table 4.4 Publishers' Frontlist E-marketing.. 72
Table 5.1 Findings Linked to Literature.. 73

Abstract

Transition from B2B to B2C Marketing in the Publishing Industry:

Modern Publishers' E-marketing Efforts

By Kim Maya Sutton

September 2011

This text focuses on business-to-consumer (B2C) e-marketing in the publishing industry. Random House CEO Dohle suggested a transition from B2B marketing to B2C marketing and Shatzkin, CEO of The Idea Logical Company, added this transition would be a good way to strengthen brands in publishing and attract loyal individual consumers. Publishers are already making varying use of the Internet and social media in 2011.

This research first analyzes existing literature on marketing and e-marketing, particularly in the publishing industry. It then focuses on seven publishers' online presence and their interaction with individual consumers on the Internet and social media, based on the author's education in computer sciences, management, and publishing.

The case study research is exploratory, phenomenological, and framed within an interpretive research paradigm. The findings are recorded in a structured dissertation, with screenshots of the relevant publishers' websites. The seven publishers are categorized according to Bernoff's stages in Managing Social Technology, and the research findings are linked back to literature, discussed, and best practices identified.

The dissertation shows that publishers are making an effort to reach their individual consumers to varying degrees and using different platforms, while remaining accessible to their trade partners, to whom they traditionally market.

As there is very little literature on B2C e-marketing in the publishing industry, this dissertation sets out to offer information on publishers' efforts in B2C e-marketing: a literature review outlines marketing in the publishing industry, and case studies illustrate seven publishers' B2C e-marketing efforts, thus contributing to closing the gap in literature on publishers' B2C e-marketing. It also sets a foundation for further research on the transition of marketing in publishing, either in qualitative case studies with publishers or quantitative research based on consumers' perception of publishers' B2C e-marketing.

Key words: publishing, marketing, B2B, B2C, e-marketing

1 Introduction

1.1 Synopsis

This dissertation focuses on marketing in the modern publishing industry, and, more specifically, publishers' current e-marketing[1] efforts to reach their consumers directly, and thus transition from a business-to-business (B2B) industry to a business-to-consumer (B2C) industry.

Publishers traditionally market and sell to the trade[2] rather than the consumer[3] (Woll 2006, p. 11), as they tend to focus their efforts towards customers who buy large volumes of books (Clark and Phillips 2008, p. 170). Shatzkin (2010) quoted Random House CEO Markus Dohle to have said

"we have to change from being a B2B company to B2C over the coming years".

Dohle allegedly elaborated that publishers need to become more reader-oriented and trendsetting while maintaining their current sales focus towards the trade. Publishers should move their focus towards consumers to strengthen their brands and thus gain long-term audiences (Shatzkin 2010). Both complementary opinions are agreeable; brands that publishers need to strengthen are books and authors, rather than the publishers themselves, to attract individual consumers and stimulate growth.

This dissertation sets out to offer information on publishers' efforts in B2C e-marketing: a literature review outlines marketing in the publishing industry, and case studies illustrate seven publishers' B2C e-marketing efforts. The discussion of the findings and conclusions identify best practices and make recommendations. This introductory chapter outlines the dissertation as a whole. After the synopsis, it gives an overview on the research background (1.2) and introduces the research problem (1.3). It then drafts the research methodology (1.4). The chapter finally describes the dissertation chapters (1.5) and concludes with the contribution of the research (1.6).

---

[1] e-marketing and e-book are hyphenated throughout this dissertation in accordance with the AP style guide 2011
[2] trade: booksellers
[3] consumer: book buyers and readers

1.2 Background to Research

Publishers often see marketing as a part of the distribution process; Bloomsbury, for example, reports marketing and distribution costs as a single, combined figure (Pallot 2011). Most publishers have a comparatively small budget for marketing (Baverstock, Bowen and Carey 2008, p. 80) and yet manage to deliver their product from the idea to the consumer. B2C marketing offers benefits to both consumer and marketer: greater price transparency, improved availability, communities with relevant information, lower marketing costs, larger marketplace, and numerous others (Solomon, Marshall and Stuart 2006, p. 507 et seq.). Bickers (2007) says that publishers are increasingly aware of the modern Internet and the fact that young people, in particular, source their information online; this research strives to find evidence for that statement on the selected publishers' Internet presences. Independent publishers can react faster to modern trends and thus succeed in B2C e-marketing, rather than cutting marketing spend and effort as the "Big Six"[4] might (Reed 2010).

To date, academic literature has lagged behind in reflecting the increasing significance of B2C marketing to publishers; very few academic publications are available on publisher's e-marketing. Relevant, up-to-date publications are most likely rare due to the topic's fast pace. General publications point out the increasing significance of modern marketing tools such as social media to reach consumers; however, to the author's knowledge, there are none that focus on publishers' B2C e-marketing endeavors. This text aims to narrow that gap by collecting and discussing e-marketing trends in the publishing industry, analyzing selected publishers' e-marketing efforts, and identifying best practices. Drawing on existing social media marketing literature, the author develops a model composed of five aspects to understand and categorize publishers' e-marketing behavior.

---

[4] The *Big Six*, the six largest publishers in the world, are Hachette, HarperCollins, MacMillan, Penguin, Random House, and Simon & Schuster (Ephron 2001, p. 240).

1.3 Research Questions

The principal research question is:

How can publishers transition from B2B marketing to B2C marketing?

This is further broken down into additional research questions:

- How can publishers make use of social media?

- How can publishers set up their websites to interest more consumers?

- What can publishers learn from other companies' transition to a B2C marketing approach?

To address these research questions, the author first analyzes existing literature, then develops a model, based on which she investigates publishers' web presences, adjusts the model in light of the case study findings, discusses the findings and identifies best practices.

1.4 Methodology

1.4.1 Research Undertaken

The case study research identifies how seven publishers interact with their consumers, and thus explores B2C e-marketing techniques used by publishers.

Qualitative research was chosen for this text to understand why and how publishers interact with their readers. A small number of cases answers the research questions holistically while allowing for the necessary detail (Denscombe 2007, p. 36; Hollensen 2004, p. 143). Following Pride's approach (2010), the research is exploratory, phenomenological, and framed within an interpretive research paradigm. Here, exploratory research is necessary to gather more information (Pride 2010, p. 133); phenomenological research allows for subjectivity, and the interpretive paradigm allows for the researcher's individual interpretation (Denscombe 2007, p. 75 et seqq.).

No ethical considerations were necessary as no direct human interaction took place for this research; the author only observed the online behavior of publishing companies as a whole.

The author collated basic information from the publishers' websites and other sources to supplement the observation, as recommended by Denscombe (2007). The author does not strive for this research to be repeatable with the same results in different cases; rather, it she intends to allow for the same results in analyzing the same cases and for them to be replicable theoretically, not statistically. The author undertook a maximum effort to ensure transparency of the case study data in the collection and analysis thereof.

The author analyzed the publishers' websites from the viewpoint of a potential consumer. The starting point was always the same: the researcher entered the publisher's name into a search engine and recorded the position therein. She then visited the publisher's website, viewing and treating it as an interested consumer. She followed links to social networks and publishers' blogs; where these did not exist, the author searched for the publisher on the most common social networking sites, namely Facebook, Twitter, and YouTube. Moreover, the author researched one book of the publishers' frontlist on the publishers' website, in social media, and from a search engine.

1.4.2 Data Collection Requirements

Cases are selected based on criteria (Denscombe 2007, p. 39). The qualifying criteria for inclusion in the research described in 1.4.1 are: a publisher must be an independent UK trade book publisher, currently involved in B2C activities, and accessible to a consumer.

1.4.3 Limitations and Researcher's Background

As the researcher collects the data (Hollensen 2004, p. 144), it is possible that her personal opinion, values, and interests influence and bias the findings. Therefore, it is important to understand her background as a "public account of ... [her]self" (Denscombe 2007, p. 69).

The author of this text is a female in her mid-thirties. She has a computer science degree and a strong interest in companies' online activities. Having helped set up several websites during the 1990s, she has followed the development of the Internet from Web 1.0 to Web 2.0 based on a professional rather than a private interest. She also has a degree in international management; therefore, this dissertation assumes that the reader has a basic understanding of (traditional) marketing and business terms. This dissertation is the major project for her Master of Arts in Publishing.

1.5 Outline of the Dissertation

The dissertation is organized into six chapters (see Table 1.1). The introductory first chapter summarizes the dissertation. It explains the research background, questions, methodology, and outline of the dissertation, as well as the contribution of the research. The next chapter is a critique of the literature. Chapter 3 introduces the conceptual model developed and used for the case study research. Chapter 4 contains the individual case studies, which are discussed in detail in chapter 5. The final chapter presents the overall conclusions, recommendations and implications for future research, and demonstrates the author's contribution to knowledge.

Table 1.1 Dissertation Outline

Dissertation Structure	Title
Chapter 1	Introduction
Chapter 2	Marketing in the Publishing Industry
Chapter 3	Conceptual Model
Chapter 4	Researched Publishers
Chapter 5	Discussion of the Findings
Chapter 6	Conclusions and Recommendations for Further Research

1.6 Contribution of Research and Conclusion

This chapter presents the research design and methodology in sufficient detail to repeat data collection.

With this text, the author contributes to knowledge by answering what publishers can do to transition from B2B to B2C marketing, and how they can use social media and their website to interact with individual consumers. An academic literature review and an analysis of relevant e-marketing trends allow for a better understanding of modern marketing in the publishing industry. This research confirms that publishers are putting effort into B2C e-marketing activities and identifies best practices.

2 Marketing in the Publishing Industry

2.1 Introduction

The purpose of this dissertation is to introduce and analyze B2C e-marketing in the publishing industry, rather than provide an exhaustive introduction to marketing, or analyze marketing theories and strategies. This second chapter descants existing literature with regard to modern marketing, publishers' marketing and modern B2C marketing.

With e-marketing becoming more prevalent, companies should make use of this efficient method to reach their consumers, target them appropriately, and convince them to become loyal customers. This would allow the company to survive in a globalizing world that floods consumers with an ever-growing variety of products.

Section 2.2 defines key terms. Section 2.3 is an introduction to marketing, 2.4 provides an overview on marketing in the publishing industry, while section 2.5 describes B2C marketing in the publishing industry, and section 2.6 outlines B2C e-marketing in the publishing industry. The conclusion in 2.7 summarizes the literature critique findings.

2.2 Key Terms Defined

Before exploring the literature, the key terms *marketing* and *publisher* must be defined, as the literature does not agree on one single definition for these terms and varies largely, depending on the source.

2.2.1 Definition of Marketing

For the purpose of this research, marketing is all market-oriented activity of a company meant to support the sale of the product to the consumer: promotion, publicity, public relations, and sales. It encompasses B2B marketing, B2C marketing, and e-marketing.

Marketing directed at business customers (here, wholesalers or book retailers) is referred to as B2B marketing and usually focuses on relationship building. Marketing directed at consumers is referred to as B2C marketing, usually focused on the consumer, and product-driven (Morva 2005).

E-marketing is any marketing effort that takes place on the Internet (Solomon, Marshall and Stuart 2006, p. 5).

Figure 2.1 illustrates how these marketing terms relate to each other.

Figure 2.1 Marketing Types and How They Relate

[source: Sutton 2011]

2.2.2 Definition of Publisher

For the purpose of this research, a publisher is a company who acquires the rights to other people's work (book, e-book, video, digital output, audio book, et cetera), or creates such a work for dissemination and distribution to a customer (wholesaler, retailer or consumer). A publisher adds value to the work by copy-editing, designing, producing, distributing and selling the work (Woll 2006, p. 8). Academic publishers, self-publishers and corporate publishers are not included in this research. This research focuses on UK publishers; however, the developed conceptual model is implementable by any modern publisher.

2.3 Introduction to Marketing

All marketing activities focus on the customer and are based on the six Rs: "offering the right people the right product by saying the right things in the right way at the right time and in the right place", while efficiently managing customer relationships (Baverstock 1997, p. 38; Solomon, Marshall and Stuart 2006, p. 6 and 569).

It is essential for companies to plan their efforts in order to be successful. Planning usually takes place in three stages and should always precede any marketing effort: strategic planning (stage 1), functional planning (stage 2), and operational planning (stage 3). Strategic planning matches the company's resources to its market opportunity (Solomon, Marshall and Stuart 2006, p. 35). Based on this strategy, the modern marketer develops a marketing program or marketing plan (Solomon, Marshall and Stuart 2006, p. 36), which ensures that efficient and effective marketing and value are delivered to the target customer (Kotler and Armstrong 2010, p. 36). Borges (2009, p. 11) states that marketing has only one purpose: to enable the sales department to fulfill their role efficiently. In stage 3, the day-to-day execution of the strategy is developed (Solomon, Marshall and Stuart 2006, p. 36).

As well as retaining existing customers, marketing is also the management of customer relations to attract new customers by offering better products than competitors and delivering satisfying products and services. Marketing is no longer a stand-alone selling and advertising function, but rather an integrated concept of satisfying customer needs, in which the marketer understands the consumer; develops a fitting product; and prices, distributes, and promotes the product effectively and relevantly (Kotler and Armstrong 2010, p. 28 et seq.; Solomon, Marshall and Stuart 2006, p. 23). This modern marketing model, also referred to as the marketing mix or the 4Ps (product, price, place, promotion), falls under functional planning and is aimed at a controlled stimulus of the consumer (Solomon, Marshall and Stuart 2006, p. 45). There is a clear differentiation between traditional marketing based on the 4 Ps, and company- and product-focused marketing. New, consumer-focused marketing is in tune with the consumer's interest. Brand recall is decreasing as consumers are desensitized from overexposure, making it difficult for brands to stand out; "360-degree marketing" is the only way for a company to stand out from the crowd and increase their own brand awareness when employing all modes possible (Blackwell 2006).

2.4 Publishers' Marketing

2.4.1 Differentiation from Other Industries

In the publishing industry, marketers play a vital role in many stages of a book's publication and become involved from the book proposal on, all the way through the entire marketing mix (Clark 2008, p. 168). However, publishers often do not have an influence on the price, place, and promotion for their product. The trade ultimately determines those (Clark 2008, p. 178 et seqq.). Nonetheless, publishers often write up complete marketing plans including the target market and its reachability (Clark 2008, p. 173). Publishers can influence the entire marketing mix only by picking trade partners carefully, adjusting contracts accordingly, and playing an active role in the B2C marketing and publicity for their products (Clark 2008, p. 179 et seq.). They can also have an influence over the entire marketing mix if they market directly to the consumer and leave out intermediaries.

Opinions in literature vary slightly but generally agree that despite this lack of influence, publishers are marketing-driven. Baverstock, Bowen and Carey (2008, p. 27) believe

> *"Publishing isn't marketing-led. It is marketing."*

Kremer (1998, p. 26) believes that marketing in publishing is a

> *"company-wide activity"*

and every function in a publishing company can and must contribute to marketing in order to make a book successful.

2.4.2 Types of Publishers' Marketing

Gardner categorized publishers' marketing efforts into seven different types (Gardner June 2011). Table 2.1 lists these categories and some examples of publishers' marketing activities within them. Gardner mentions that publishers usually have a sales team selling books to book retailers and other stores and, contradictory to the definition in section 2.2.1, states that this is not a classical marketing function.

Table 2.1 Publishers' Marketing Efforts

Category	Example of Publishers' Marketing Activity Within Category
Promotional activities	writing blurb copy, creating press kits
Trade advertising	placement in retailers' catalogues, advertisements in trade magazines and with distributors, in-store promotion
Internet marketing	working with online booksellers, helping the author create a presence on social media
Internet advertising	ads on social media, banners on relevant sites
Specialized promotions	book clubs, reading groups, submission to prizes
Trade publicity	trade shows, trade magazine reviews
Consumer publicity	book tours, interviews, press releases, influencer copies

[source: Sutton 2011, based on Gardner June 2011]

2.4.3 Marketing Expenditure and Target Audience

Marketing expenditure is highly dependent on the expected sales revenue of a book, and must always be recouped; it is often budgeted to be a percentage of anticipated sales (Baverstock 1997, p. 215). The Internet offers considerable marketing potential, enabling a publisher's marketer to reach relevant target audiences cost-efficiently (Clark and Phillips 2008, p. 168), provided the marketer knows his audience (Zarrella 2011, p. 115). However, e-marketing cannot conceal a bad product (Myers 2009); offering a decent product in the proper fashion to the right customer is most important. In 2006, HarperCollins became one of the first publishers to recruit help from outside the publishing industry to maximize their efforts and resulting opportunities in the digital field (Bone 2006); they realized that a fresh look and experience unrelated to the industry would be helpful.

The next sections look at publishers' traditional B2C marketing and B2C e-marketing.

2.5 Traditional B2C Marketing in the Publishing Industry

In publishing, several traditional tools can be used to market directly to the consumer: the brand, the book design itself, media attention, reading initiatives, book prizes, and viral marketing (Clark and Phillips 2008, p. 168 et seqq.). All these elements can also be implemented into a publisher's e-marketing campaign.

2.5.1 Brand

Brands encourage the consumer's ability to recognize and differentiate a product and increase brand awareness. Increased brand awareness leads to easier promotion of the product (Hollensen 2004, p. 470).

In publishing, there are three types of brands: the author or content provider, the literature, and the publisher. To the consumer, the publishers' brand is not as recognizable and thus not as relevant to their buying decision as other consumer brands may be. Brand names in publishing, however, influence trade intermediaries (Clark and Phillips 2008, p. 173). The author's brand is a strong marketing tool; he[5] can help promote the book, as he is most

---

[5] References to the male gender are for simplification and apply to both males and females.

knowledgeable, passionate, and directly involved (Hyatt 2011; Gardner August 2, 2011). The reader would rather connect with the author (Gardner August 16, 2011) than the publisher. The successful self-publisher John Locke has proven that branding and successful communication with the target audience can take place on many platforms, most currently on e-marketing platforms, such as blogs and Facebook (Shatzkin 2011a), and that this can boost sales, and turn readers into loyal fans and followers. These two aspects are the aim of every marketing effort.

2.5.2 Book Design

Book design is closely related to the content provider as a brand, as readers need to be able to quickly identify what type of book by which content creator they are looking at. The book's design thus helps to position it; it often differs in separate markets (Clark and Phillips 2008, p. 176 et seqq.). For e-marketing, this can be even more crucial as consumers often browse with less time online than in traditional retail stores.

2.5.3 Media Attention

Sometimes, publishers do not control marketing, as with the recent article on Jon-Jon Goulian's memoir *The Man in the Gray Flannel Skirt* (Bertodano 2011). The article is not a review or an excerpt, but rather an interview with the author. The extract *Tabasco with Everything* (Birnbaum 2011) in *The Guardian Weekend* is not labeled as an advertisement, nor is it an interview or review; rather, it is an edited excerpt from the book *Season to Taste* by Molly Birnbaum. At the end of the excerpt, the reader finds information on where to obtain the book. These two examples show that marketing can take place without the publisher's initiative. Publishers do try to influence this by creating a list of potential relevant reviewers to whom they send books, with a request for a review printed in the reviewer's publication (Clark and Phillips 2008, p. 187 et seq.). This too can be utilized for e-marketing, as publishers can enter into relationships with online magazines and bloggers.

2.5.4 Reading Initiatives and Prizes

Publishers are aware of the need to encourage the public's reading. They encourage and participate in events. Canongate's CEO Byng, for example, started the World Book Night in

2011, and almost two dozen publishers participate in World Book Day[6] in the UK. Publishers who participate in reading initiatives should integrate their participation into their e-marketing strategies.

Richardson (2008) points out that some book prizes and awards attract attention and media coverage. Thus, publishers should integrate awards into their e-marketing strategies and cross-promote, for example, the Man Booker Prize when they get listed.

2.5.5 Viral Marketing

Word-of-mouth marketing, or viral marketing, is very helpful for boosting sales. Although hardly any company can start a successful viral campaign, publishers can foster viral marketing by supporting book clubs and reading groups (Richardson 2008, p. 37). Publishers can also attempt to gain media coverage and prominent placement in bookstores to intensify word-of-mouth campaigns (Clark and Phillips 2008, p. 181), but these methods can be costly. Other ways to start viral marketing are content creator tours and appearances at literary festivals (Clark and Phillips 2008, p. 181), which can also be costly and time-consuming. The Internet, however, offers great opportunities to advertise, generate attention, and create interest (Clark and Phillips 2008, p. 181); social networking sites are the perfect place to start what Zarella (2011, p. 113) refers to as

> *"contagious campaigns"*.

2.6 B2C E-marketing in the Publishing Industry

2.6.1 Introduction

Recent developments in technology have changed companies' requirements dramatically. Companies must now react much faster to deliver value to their customers. However, these new developments also give companies new methods to understand and communicate with their customers individually or in groups (Solomon, Marshall and Stuart 2006, p. 405; Thompson p. 315). More than 1.2 billion Internet users worldwide spend nearly half their time online looking at content and one third of their online time communicating with friends;

---

[6] World Book Day is a yearly event occurring on April 23. It was established in 1995 and is organized by UNESCO.

it is thus no surprise that online marketing, also referred to as e-marketing, is the fastest-growing form of marketing (Kotler and Armstrong 2010, p. 48 et seqq.). Companies can lose their place in the market if they do not manage to keep up with the changes (Newlands 2011, Introduction); conversely, if they make use of technology, they can incorporate support forums for customers and proactively market their products (Thompson 2005, p. 315). Kotler (2011) points out the importance that companies shift more promotion to digital forms in order to get the consumers to talk about the product online, preferably well.

With the rise of "e-tailers" such as Amazon (Thompson 2005, p. 315; Hall 2011) and the closure of traditional book stores (Campbell 2011b and 2011c), publishers who want to shift their focus to B2C marketing should also increase their e-marketing.

2.6.2 Online Consumers' Needs

Companies need to understand their target market; they need to know exactly where their consumers spend time and what they do. One way to find out is by engaging them in the relevant forums with appreciated content (Borges 2009, p. 15). Dell, for example, has successfully set up social media microblogging channels on www.sina.com in order to build awareness among students and young professionals in China. Within less than six months, Dell became the third most-followed brand and changed the way international brands talk to their customers with relevant content (SNCR 2011).

Borges (2009) and Zarrella, (2011) point out that consumers primarily want relationships with the companies they buy from. Consumers want to be heard and see that their feedback is implemented.

2.6.3 Publishers' Websites

E-marketing has changed the face of marketing and promotion. Publishers' websites usually have a very comprehensive marketing function, as information on their titles becomes publically available. Books can be ordered via the website, and websites can be enhanced with additional information and interactive content, such as author interviews and games linked to books, where appropriate (Clark 2008, p. 180; Thompson 2005). Most importantly, the publisher's website is a way to get in touch and stay in contact with consumers (Clark 2008, p. 181). Websites can also be used to highlight events, such as readings or performances, make coupons available, and offer benefits to consumers who bought an item in a physical store (Hollensen 2004, p. 378 et seq.). In summary, a publisher's website must fulfill three tasks: provide ecommerce facilities, build relationships with consumers, and enhance brand awareness (Sayce, 2011).

2.6.4 Social Media and Blogs

Companies favor social media channels as efficient, effective and less costly (Reed 2010) over traditional mass media channels for promoting their products and news. These new channels involve the consumer and influence how they relate to product and brand. Companies can be most successful when they create a community that provides more than functional benefits: platforms where the company listens to the consumer and implements suggested changes (Aaker 2011; Zarrella 2011 p. 7). HarperCollins, for example, has started *authonomy*, a writing community for readers, writers, agents, and publishers to show and discuss writing (*authonomy* 2011).

Internet platforms are now forums in which users create value (Shuen 2008). Gunelius and Shuen have moved away from the term consumer, and coined "prosumer" instead; prosumer captures the consumer's influence on products via social media (Gunelius 2011, p. 25; Shuen 2008, p. 1). Harnessing network effects and collective intelligence is referred to as the Web 2.0 (Shuen 2008, p. x); the Internet is transformed into a platform with applications that improve with more people using them and giving their feedback (O'Reilly in Shuen 2008, p. xvii). Ian Davies (2005) explained Web 2.0 as such:

> "Web 2.0 is an attitude not a technology. It's about enabling and encouraging participation through open applications and services. By open I mean technically open [...] but also, more importantly, socially open, with rights granted to use the content in new and exciting contexts."

Companies that do not just publish but also implement user participation are key dominators in the Web 2.0 (O'Reilly 2005). For example, on www.anobii.com and www.goodreads.com, publishers can become active and foster relationships with readers through the existing social media sites Facebook and Twitter, so that other readers can find, share and discuss (Neill 2011); the publishers can thus "harness collective intelligence" (O'Reilly 2005), and acquire new customers (Miller 2011). Implementing user participation can also help with receiving reviews and thus publicizing books (Roberts 2011).

As social media grows dramatically, failing to bridge the gap between the buyer and seller through social media platforms would be potentially dangerous for a business (Borges 2009, p. 9). The time commitment necessary for the engagement with individual consumers can be a disadvantage; independent publishers are more likely to endure this (Reed 2010).

2.6.5 Stages of Managing Social Technology

Bernoff (2011) categorized companies' efforts in managing social technology; Table 2.2 summarizes his research. These stages illustrate the transition a company must undergo from not being active with social technology to having mastered it entirely. The case studies examined in chapter 4 are categorized using Bernoff's stages.

Table 2.2 Bernoff's Stages of Managing Social Technology

Stage	Company's Behavior
I: dormant	not yet involved in social media
II: testing	company has pilots on social media sites
III: coordinating	formal policies get set up
IV: scaling and optimizing	companies are no longer just listening, but efficiently moving to new ideas from customers such as www.MyStarbucksIdea.com
V: empowered	internal and external social applications around the world such as at Dell

[source: Sutton 2011, based on Bernoff 2011]

2.6.6 Other Trends

The Internet shows several other e-marketing trends in the publishing industry. This list is not exhaustive; it merely identifies some trends and their possible usefulness to publishers.

2.6.6.1 Gardners' Hive

A good example of how a supplier (wholesaler) and an intermediary (retailer) work together to target the consumer relevantly and effectively is the launch of UK wholesaler Gardners' website *Hive* in June 2011. It directly addresses consumers and allows them to shop locally over the Internet, while the participating retailer closest to the consumer receives remuneration, depending on whether the consumer has the item shipped to their home (5%) or delivered to the retailer (10%) (Campbell 2011a). A similar website for publishers might be successful as well.

2.6.6.2 Involving Authors

Publishers who involve authors in building an authentic online presence allow for the exploitation of the authors' knowledge about their audience and the subject. The Independent Alliance[7] offers their authors blogging workshops (Reed 2010). Authors should be encouraged to build their online presence on all channels appropriate for the genre and engage in relevant forums as well.

2.6.6.3 Other Online Networks

Participation in other online networks such as *Second Life* can help niche publishers become known faster, while inducing low to no costs (Reed 2010). Starting dedicated online networks or games can lead to viral campaigns (Ronai 2009) and even be used for the sole purpose of marketing following a general "gamification" (Kalder 2011) trend; this might generate high costs and thus must be considered carefully within the marketing strategy and budget. It is also important to consider that consumers might notice that the gamification is simply a marketing method and might be put off by the publisher's effort.

2.6.6.4 Affinity Schemes

Publishers can tie reciprocal affinity schemes into their e-marketing campaigns: the consumer receives a benefit, often monetary, and the publisher receives the consumer's data in return based on which closer targeted interaction between publisher and consumer becomes possible.

Several booksellers have affinity schemes already: Waterstone's Reward Card, and Blackwell's Rewards. These offer a monetary benefit between a 3% and a 5% discount, and exclusive extras such event tickets, or participation in competitions.

Outside the publishing industry, there are numerous affinity schemes throughout the UK: the Nectar system (2% discount redeemable with many different retailers), the Tesco Club card, the Boots Advantage card, and many more. This shows that consumers are used to affinity schemes and that publishers could benefit from setting up something similar.

---

[7] The Independent Alliance is a global alliance of ten UK publishers led by Faber & Faber.

2.6.6.5 E-books

Marketing an e-book is different from marketing a traditional book in that consumers never buy e-books in traditional retail stores, but rather online at e-tailers such as Amazon, Waterstone's, and play.com. E-books have to have proper metadata and the publisher needs to optimize e-books for search engines so that consumers can find them. All other e-marketing equally applies to e-books. Marketing e-books properly requires technical knowledge that publishers might have to acquire from outside the publishing industry (Shatzkin 2011b).

2.6.6.6 Odyl

Odyl is a Facebook application designed to help authors and publishers connect with readers on Facebook. Odyl alleges on their website that they work with several big publishers via Facebook; however, all publishers' appearances on the Odyl website are just logos and there are no links to click through to the allegedly participating publishers. Following some of the linked websites reveals that the Odyl application is a collection of information on the publishers', author's or book's Facebook fanpage which can only be accessed and seen after the visitor clicks the *Like* button and thus becomes connected with the product, receiving regular status updates (Odyl 2011; Facebook 2011).

2.7 Conclusion

Publishers should make use of all opportunities the Internet offers. They might otherwise risk losing business by not adapting fast enough or not gaining online business by not reaching their consumers. Publishers who focus their entire marketing efforts towards the book trade and not the consumer might make a mistake, particularly in the modern age of e-marketing.

From the literature critique in chapter 2 emerges a clearer understanding of modern B2C e-marketing. The focus of this chapter is on e-marketing methods suitable for publishers to reach their consumers and succeed in the 21st century. Publishers innately create content and should be able to deliver this content to their consumers in a relevant and accessible fashion. As a rising number of people are active online, publishers who are also active online and provide information on their products in relevant forums have an advantage over those who do not.

It is apparent that modern companies need to embrace technology, become involved in what is sometimes referred to as the Web 2.0, and allow for users to interact with the company in order to create value that is truly appreciated by and relevant to the consumer. Publishers who market directly to the consumer have full control over the entire marketing mix; therefore, publishers should focus on both the consumer and the business customer. Publishers must understand where their consumers are so that they can target them appropriately. To reach consumers who spend a significant amount of their time online, e-marketing is the most appropriate and state-of-the-art method. Publishers should also use traditional B2C marketing methods to reach consumers who are not active online, and incorporate these methods into their e-marketing strategy. This would increase the number of consumers reached and enhance brand awareness.

The next chapter introduces the model developed for this research, and chapter 4 examines what exactly the chosen publishers have already implemented at the time of research.

3 Conceptual Model

3.1 Introduction

Chapter 2 examines literature on modern marketing; it distinguishes publishers' marketing, and clarifies traditional B2C approaches used by publishers. Chapter 2 also introduces publishers' B2C e-marketing methods and trends. However, despite the descriptions laid out in chapter 2, there are limitations to our understanding of modern publishers' B2C marketing opportunities. To the author's knowledge, no research has been undertaken as to what publishers have already incorporated.

Section 3.2 introduces the model developed; it includes Figure 3.1, which shows the model as it is used for the research of the case studies. Section 3.3 describes the limitations of this model, followed by a conclusion.

3.2 Current Publishers' B2C Marketing

In order to examine which marketing activities publishers currently pursue, the author developed a model based on the literature critique, after not finding a specific existing conceptual model that could have served as a basis. This new theory-based model can be used for classifying publishers' marketing activities. It contains five aspects:

- content provider,
- publisher,
- website (publisher's and content provider's),
- e-marketing (Web 2.0), and
- consumer response.

This model aims to give insight into the interplay of these five aspects in creating a platform for a modern consumer active online. The aspects website and e-marketing shed light on the publishers' use of social media and changing the publishers' website into a more direct website (research questions 2 and 3). The model also helps to build an understanding of what publishers might learn from other companies (research question 4).

Figure 3.1 Publishers' B2C Activities

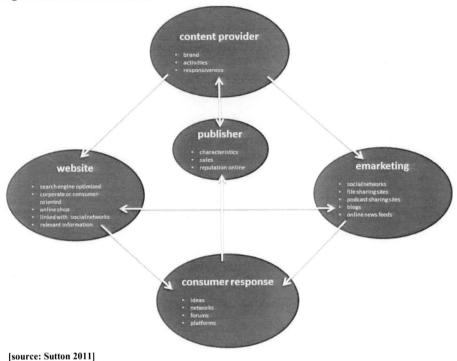

[source: Sutton 2011]

Finally, this model as a whole gives insight into the independent publishers' transition from B2B to B2C marketing (research question 1).

The **content provider** is the most important figure in this model. Without a content provider, the publisher would have no material to publish. Content provider and publisher work closely together to create a brand around the content provider and his work. The brand is fostered through activities, such as content creator tours (virtual or actual), and forum participation. A highly responsive content provider, particularly in e-marketing efforts, makes himself visible, credible and authentic.

The aspect **publisher** covers the publisher's characteristics as per the data collection requirements, as well as additional characteristics, such as sales numbers where available and the publisher's online reputation in numbers of friends/ followers. The publisher is ideally influenced by the **consumer response**.

The aspects **website** and **e-marketing** focus on the publishers' behavior and appearance in their attempt to build brand awareness around their own brand and that of the content provider and his work. Both aspects are interlinked and influence each other. The publishers' websites and their e-marketing attempts become communication platforms that give consumers a chance to interact and respond to the publishers' output.

3.3 Limitations of this Model

This model is the basis to understanding publishers' e-marketing efforts, incorporating knowledge from Clark and Philips (2008) and Baverstock, Bowen and Carey (2008). The model only concerns publishers' online B2C activities. It is used as an organizing, thought-ordering model; it is not intended to be deterministic or fit for quantitative testing. It is also not possible to separate causality from correlation with this model. After the discussion of the findings in chapter 5, this model may have to be adjusted to include the analysis.

3.4 Conclusion

The use of this model is justifiable as it draws on various literatures. As no similar research has been undertaken, a new model had to be devised. This model is applied to case studies (chapter 4), in which each publisher is examined in regards to these different aspects in order to get a better picture of publishers' B2C e-marketing activities and similarities across the seven selected publishers.

4 Researched Publishers

4.1 Introduction

The publishers analyzed in this research are of various genres. The selection has been made based on the data collection requirements outlined in 1.4.2. The broadness of the sample is purposeful, due to the exploratory nature of the research; a broad sample gives the most insight into different publishers' e-marketing efforts.

This chapter first gives an overview on the seven case studies in section 4.2. Section 4.3 examines each of the case studies as to the publishers' B2C e-marketing and frontlist e-marketing efforts based on one randomly selected book. A cross-case analysis in section 4.4 including a summary of the publishers' B2C efforts in Table 4.2 rounds off the chapter. The conclusion of the case study findings is in section 4.5.

This chapter aims to answer the research question of what publishers can do to transition to a more consumer-oriented marketing (research question 1) by identifying best practices that facilitate successful modern B2C e-marketing. Chapter 5 contains the discussion of the findings.

4.2 Overview of Publishers

Table 4.1 provides an overview of all case studies, profiling them by providing the name, founding year, the publisher's website and the frontlist title selected for the frontlist e-marketing. All publishers were listed on the first position in Google when searching for the full publisher's name.

Table 4.1 Case Profiles

Publisher Name	Founding Year	Website	Frontlist Title
Salt Publishing	1999	www.saltpublishing.com	Fred Sedgwick *Here Comes the Poetry Man* (February 2011)
Nosy Crow	2010	www.nosycrow.com	Sue Ransom *Small Blue Thing* (January 2011)
PS Publishing	1999	www.pspublishing.co.uk	Jack Dann *Junction* (April 2011)
Gollancz Science Fiction	1998	www.orionbooks.co.uk/genres/sf-fantasy	Adam Robert *By Light Alone* (August 2011)
Bloomsbury	1986	www.bloomsbury.com	Stephen Kelman *Pigeon English* (March 2011)
Portobello Books	2005	www.portobellobooks.com	Molly Birnbaum *Season To Taste* (August 2011)
Canongate Books	1973	www.canongate.tv	Helen Walsh *Go to Sleep* (July 2011)

[source: Sutton 2011]

4.3 In-Depth Case Profiles

The seven case studies are recorded following the same pattern. First, a general publisher's profile introduces the publisher and their e-marketing strategy where available. Subsection 2 describes the publisher's website from a visitor's viewpoint. Subsection 3 outlines the publisher's social media usage; while subsection 4 looks at the publisher's consumer response. Subsection 5 introduces the selected frontlist book e-marketing, and subsection 6 provides a short summary of the respective case study.

4.3.1 Salt Publishing

4.3.1.1 Publisher Profile

Salt Publishing (Salt) is an independent publisher in England, focusing on poetry, literary fiction, and short stories. Based in Cromer, Norfolk, they publish around 80 books per year, were founded in 1999 and are now represented in the UK, the USA, New Zealand and Australia. The core team at Salt comprises of two directors plus two editors in the UK, and commissioning editors in the USA and Australia (Salt 2011). Salt had a 72% increase in sales in 2007, after ceasing all marketing except for e-marketing (Reed 2010). In 2009, Salt managed to start a viral campaign "Just One Book", with which they asked their followers to support them after having lost significant funding form the Arts Council (Ronai, 2009).

4.3.1.2 Website

Salt claims on their page that they have more than 25 million page visits per year from over 600,000 visitors, of which roughly one third comes from the UK, one third from the USA and the rest of the visitors from over 100 countries worldwide (Salt 2011).

The website (Figure 4.1) is a mixture of information for consumers and trade customers. It contains newsworthy items, information on distribution, links to social networking sites, and a link to an online magazine hosted by Salt. A navigation bar (Figure 4.2) makes Salt's authors, list, advertising campaign, prizes, and other options easily accessible for the visitor. The news button in the navigational bar leads the user to the Salt blog, which feeds directly and seemingly automatically into Facebook and Twitter. Within the blog, the user can filter by categories or click on one specific news item in a list of recent posts (Figure 4.3).

4.3.1.3 Social Media

Salt's main website invites visitors to associate with Salt via an array of mediums (Figure 4.4). Following these links, visitors can mention Salt's respective site on their own social networking pages and thus recommend Salt books.

Salt's webpage, however, is lacking links to connect with Salt on social networking sites; the interested consumer has to search for Salt on social media sites. Salt comes up as the first link on Twitter when searching "Salt Publishing" (Figure 4.5). On Facebook as well, Salt has a page presence that consumers can like and thus follow (Figure 4.6). Salt is communicating similar information on both Twitter and Facebook: primarily news about publications, new arrivals at the Salt office, participation in literary events and prizes won by Salt. Additionally, they communicate news they consider relevant to their readers (Figure 4.7).

A search on YouTube reveals a channel run by Salt Publishing (Figure 4.8) to which they upload advertising campaigns, author interviews, and videos from launch parties and other events.

4.3.1.4 Consumer Response

In addition to the comprehensive contact information available via the navigation bar, Salt provides a recommendation feature with which consumers can recommend a new author to be published by Salt (Figure 4.9), and thus actively influence the publisher's list. The publisher's involvement on Facebook, Twitter and their blog shows that they take consumer response seriously. They react to almost all responses and show their appreciation by letting the consumer feel that they listen to them; however, there is no evidence that Salt implements any reader's ideas.

4.3.1.5 Frontlist E-marketing

Sedgwick's book *Here Comes the Poetry Man* is listed on Salt's main website. Following the link, the visitor receives information on Sedgwick and a sample poem from the book. There are no social media connections for the visitor to follow for more information, nor are there any links to connect with the author, neither on the publisher's website nor in a search engine. Sedgwick does not seem to have a presence on social media.

4.3.1.6 Summary Salt Publishing

A very engaging website together with presences across all common social media platforms enables Salt to communicate closely with their readers. The information provided targets their core audience, and thus centers on poetry and literary fiction. Salt responds to their readers and has a loyal following on Facebook and Twitter. Their innovative e-marketing campaign "Just One Book" and its impact are unmatched, and show they have a caring fan base. The fact that Salt only markets online sets them apart from other publishers; their frontlist author could be better integrated into Salt's e-marketing.

Figure 4.1 Salt Main Webpage

Figure 4.2 Salt Navigation Bar

Figure 4.3 Salt Blog Categories and Recent Posts

Figure 4.4 Salt Social Media Links

Figure 4.5 Salt on Twitter

Figure 4.6 Salt on Facebook

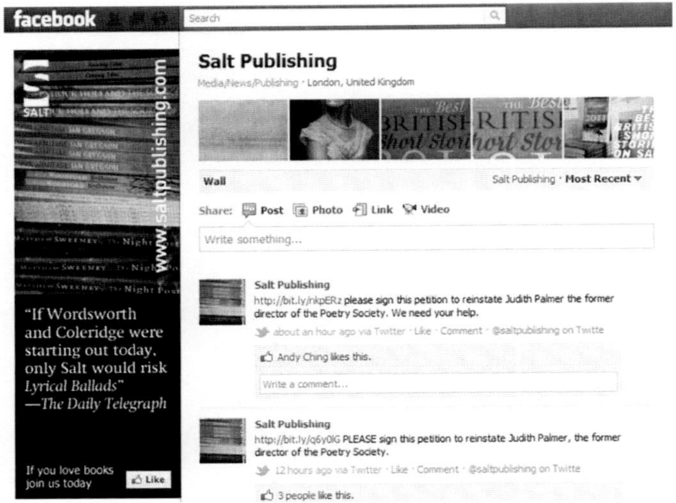

Figure 4.7 Salt News

Salt Publishing
Reports coming in of a huge terrorist attack in Norway.
July 22 at 6:05pm via Twitter · Like · Comment · @saltpublishing on Twitter

Figure 4.8 Salt on YouTube

Figure 4.9 Recommendation to Salt

My recommendation

Help us discover great new talent by telling us about writers you think we should add to our list. We love hearing about your discoveries, so take five minutes to let us know who you think is worth publishing and where we can find them.

Please fill in all fields marked with a *

About me

1. My name *

2. My email address *

About the author

3. What is the author's name?

4. Do you have any contact details?

About the author's work

5. What do you like about the work?

6. Is there anything else you can tell us?

4.3.2 Nosy Crow

4.3.2.1 Publisher Profile

Nosy Crow is an independent London-based publisher for children's books and applications. Upon foundation, Nosy Crow employed four staff members and grew within a year to a team of twelve people plus one freelance publicist (Horn 2010; Nosy Crow 2011). Originally, Nosy Crow planned fifteen to twenty inaugural titles (Horn 2010); they actually published twenty-three books within the first two years (Nosy Crow 2011). Founder Wilson said that Nosy Crow "is free of the constraints of… a corporate structure" (Horn 2010).

4.3.2.2 Website

Nosy Crow's website appearance seems to target a younger audience, and yet has all the information an adult visitor might be looking for. The navigation bar leads to Nosy Crow's blog integrated in the website, an information page about their history and employees, their books and applications, authors, news and reviews, contact information, and a media kit for writers, journalists, and bloggers looking for more information (Figure 4.12). The main page also displays current articles ("We've got something to crow about!"), recent blog posts, a list of events where readers can meet Nosy Crow and their team or authors, and some media coverage on Nosy Crow. The website has a mixture of pictures, text, embedded videos, interviews, and graphics (Nosy Crow 2011).

4.3.2.3 Social Media

Nosy Crow invites the visitor to follow them on the social media applications Facebook, Twitter and YouTube. The reader can also conveniently access Nosy Crow's RSS feed (Figure 4.13).

Nosy Crow's Facebook presence also targets primarily an older audience, parents, teachers, and possibly trade customers. The publisher's description has several typographical errors. The Facebook presence does not offer any fun applications, despite Nosy Crow claiming that they "actively embrace new technology in what [they] make, and in how [they] tell people about it" (Nosy Crow 2011). Nosy Crow has linked their blog entries to appear automatically as soon as they are posted; otherwise, Nosy Crow lists a few items as recommendations and posts news articles.

4.3.2.4 Consumer Response

On Facebook, Nosy Crow does not always respond to consumers comments, and even when they do, the often do after more than one day. Nosy Crow does engage in conversation with other Twitter users. On the contact website, there is a general email address for queries. This is targeted at trade customers (Figure 4.11).

4.3.2.5 Frontlist E-marketing

Ransom's book *Small Blue Things* is the first of a trilogy and was the first publication by Nosy Crow. It has its own dedicated website (www.smallbluething.com) with the book's video trailer. On this website, the visitor receives relevant news and information on media coverage, as well as the chance to connect to the book on Facebook, follow the author on Twitter, and sign up for newsletters. The publisher's webpage links to the dedicated book webpage (Figure 4.10), which also links back to the publisher's webpage. The book's page on Facebook (188 fans) has several comments by the author who also has a fan page (35 fans). No author blog was found when conducting an online research. Nosy Crow built up a following for the book on Twitter a few weeks leading up to the publication date (Nosy Crow 2011).

4.3.2.6 Summary Nosy Crow

Nosy Crow built up a steadily increasing following during their first two years of trading and created a fresh online presence that integrates most available social applications.

However, despite Nosy Crow being a children's publisher, their presence seems aimed at an older audience and trade customers. There is a lack of age appropriate entertainment on their website and social media presence; the information written on the blog also targets an older audience.

Figure 4.12 Nosy Crow Main Webpage

Figure 4.10 Nosy Crow Links to Frontlist Book

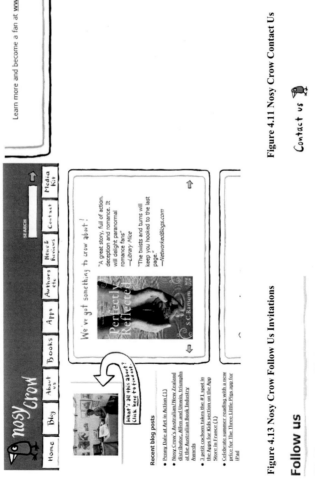

Figure 4.11 Nosy Crow Contact Us

Figure 4.13 Nosy Crow Follow Us Invitations

4.3.3 PS Publishing

4.3.3.1 Publisher Profile

Established in 1999 with the aim to publish high-quality science fiction, fantasy and horror books, PS Publishing (PS) has published over 260 books to date. They have received several awards over the years, such as six times the British Fantasy Awards for the Best Small Press (PS 2011). PS specializes in publishing fantasy, science fiction, and horror novellas.

4.3.3.2 Website

PS' website is importunate and confusing. The very large logo dominates the page; a three-line navigation bar almost vanishes under it (Figure 4.14). A very busy collection of pictures is set up to link to PS's novels, novellas, forthcoming titles, et cetera (Figure 4.17).

PS's website features an online shop; visitors can add all books on the site to the shopping cart conveniently, quickly check out and pay for their shopping via PayPal and several credit cards.

Links to connect to PS on social media are at the bottom of the website (Figure 4.18).

4.3.3.3 Social Media

The Facebook link supplied on PS's website directs the visitor to the Facebook profile of Peter Crowther, one of two founders of PS, without explanation of this correlation. Crowther's Facebook page is not a company fan page, but rather an individual user page. Visitors can share individual book pages on the PS website on Facebook email them to friends.

The Twitter link leads to PS's company Twitter presence; the posts here are very sporadic. The blog button routes the visitor to Crowther's blog, which was established in July 2011 and has four entries to date. The YouTube button leads to the main page of YouTube; PS does not have a channel set up, and there are very few movies tagged with PS (Figure 4.15).

4.3.3.4 Consumer Response

The invitation "enquiries regarding sales, order processing, returns, or general enquiries" (PS 2011) targets the trade rather than consumers. An attempt to contact Peter Crowther revealed that he does not react to Facebook friend requests for weeks, so an interested consumer trying to get in contact this way will not get any additional information quickly.

The PS website does allow consumers to write reviews for all individual books after setting up an account with PS (Figure 4.16). Visitors can get this account only during an order process with PS.

4.3.3.5 Frontlist E-marketing

Dann's book *Junction* is listed in the novels section of PS' website. There are no links to any social media connection with the author, or to any external author or book websites. Jack Dann has no active Facebook fan page or Twitter account. His blog (www.jackdann.com) is listed first in search engines when searching "Jack Dann author"; it is not linked to from PS' website, while Dann does link back to PS.

4.3.3.6 Summary PS Publishing

PS Publishing is marketing primarily to the trade and not very engaged with B2C e-marketing. Several options are set up, but PS does not seem to integrate them actively yet.

Figure 4.14 PS Main Webpage

Figure 4.15 PS Tagged on YouTube

Figure 4.17 PS Links

Figure 4.16 PS Book Review

Figure 4.18 PS Social Networking Links

4.3.4 Gollancz

4.3.4.1 Publisher Profile

Gollancz is the science fiction and fantasy imprint of the London-based Orion Publishing Group Limited (Orion), which is part of French Hachette Livre (Herbert 2010). Orion was founded in 1991 and acquired Victor Gollancz Ltd. in 1998. Gollancz has a range of known authors and publishes individual books, including the Science Fiction and Fantasy Masterworks series (Gollancz 2011).

4.3.4.2 Website

As Gollancz is an Orion imprint, visitors searching for Gollancz in a search engine find the Orion webpage (www.orionbooks.co.uk/genres/sf-fantasy) as the publisher's designated imprint page. Gollancz' website follows Orion's corporate identity (Figure 4.19). There is no online shop; instead, books can be purchased by following links to play.com, Waterstone's, Amazon, and The Book Depository.

The books on the Orion webpage are not listed by imprint; their default listing is sorted by publication date and can be limited to just Gollancz books by entering *Gollancz* as a keyword in the search.

4.3.4.3 Social Media

The main Orion webpage and the imprint pages contain no social media links. Finding a Facebook link for Gollancz is difficult on the Orion website; there is one for Gollancz Dark Fantasy, following the True Blood feature from the main website (Figure 4.20). Gollancz has two pages on Facebook, one for Gollancz and one for Gollancz Dark Fantasy. These pages contain mainly post competitions and YouTube videos for author interviews and trailers. Most videos linked on YouTube are uploaded by the YouTube user *orionbooks*, for whom there is also a YouTube channel. YouTube has no Gollancz channel. The Gollancz blog does not allow for user interaction, comments, or feedback. Gollancz' has a Twitter account and regularly posts and interacts.

4.3.4.4 Consumer Response

The *Contact-Us* page is very basic; it contains some *Frequently Asked Questions*, links for publicity, rights and permission enquiries, and information for trade orders. There is no special consumer response forum or tool.

There are several consumer comments on the Gollancz Facebook pages that did not get responses from Gollancz (examples are Figure 4.21, Figure 4.22, and Figure 4.23).

4.3.4.5 Frontlist E-marketing

Robert's *By Light Alone* is listed on Gollancz' main website; the interested visitor can follow a link to the author's blog (www.adamroberts.com) about his books, book reviews, events and appearances, and more. Roberts can be found on Twitter as well; his Facebook page is a user page instead of a fan page and he does not seem to accept friend requests from fans.

4.3.4.6 Summary Gollancz

Gollancz' online presence is aimed at trade customers and their engagement with B2C e-marketing is minimal at this point. Several social media accounts have been set up but are sparsely used and with no apparent overall strategy. Gollancz does not regularly engage with consumers, and leaves questions unanswered. Gollancz' could tie in their authors' social media presences more effectively.

Figure 4.21 Gollancz Facebook Conversation One

Figure 4.19 Gollancz Main Webpage

Figure 4.22 Gollancz Facebook Conversation Two

Figure 4.23 Gollancz Facebook Conversation Three

Figure 4.20 Gollancz Dark Fantasy Social Media

4.3.5 Bloomsbury

4.3.5.1 Publisher Profile

Bloomsbury Publishing Plc (Bloomsbury) is an independent London-based publisher founded in 1986 in the UK and now represented in the UK, USA, Germany, and Australia. Following several acquisitions since 2002, Bloomsbury has four divisions since March 2011: Academic and Professional Publishing, Information, Adult Publishing, and Children's Publishing. In 2007, Bloomsbury had a market share of 4.2% in the UK (Clark and Phillips 2008, p. 25). For fourteen months ending February 2011, Bloomsbury reports revenue of over £100 million (Bloomsbury 2011). Clark and Phillips attribute Bloomsbury's growth largely to the Harry Potter series (2008, p. 29).

4.3.5.2 Website

Bloomsbury's main website (Figure 4.24) hosts a mixture of information for consumers and trade, easily discernible in the navigation bar.

The website contains prize information, a Twitter feed, author news, publishing news, embedded videos, reading group guides, sneak peeks, links to author and book blogs, a bestseller list, links to the online bookshop, and linked buttons to follow Bloomsbury on social media.

At the bottom of the page is additional information about Bloomsbury, career opportunities at Bloomsbury, and information for investors (Figure 4.25), as well as a group of links on The Bloomsbury Group.

The outside frames of the website remain the same and only the content in the middle of the window changes depending on the category (authors, news, events, et cetera). When navigating to Children's or Harry Potter, the entire look of the website changes to match the new target audience (Figure 4.26 and Figure 4.27), and a new category becomes available: Fun Stuff.

The Harry Potter website has a different, dedicated URL as well (harrypotter.bloomsbury.com). This website is on position 7 when searched for in a search engine.

In the new fun stuff category of the Harry Potter website, there are several games, printable bookmarks, and posters. The author, J.K. Rowling, also announces the new Pottermore experience in a video on this website, in which she talks about "an online reading experience unlike any other... with a few crucial additions... the most important one is you... so Pottermore will be built in part by you" (Rowling 2011). Bloomsbury's Children's website also has additional content: downloadable coloring-in sheets, activity packs, and games.

4.3.5.3 Social Media

Bloomsbury invites visitors to follow them on Twitter and YouTube (Figure 4.28), and to order their books online from the public library. The fourth offered link, presumably another social media link, is not functional.

There is no presence for Bloomsbury on Facebook.

There are no options on the main Bloomsbury website to share information on any social media site; the individual book pages however can be shared through social media (Figure 4.29).

4.3.5.4 Consumer Response

Independently from Bloomsbury, J.K. Rowling has responded to her fan base sending tremendous amounts of ideas, drawings, letters, and pictures by setting up Pottermore. She gives readers the opportunity to interact, shape the website and have a new reading experience with Harry Potter. Harry Potter e-books will be available only through this platform (Flood 2011), although Bloomsbury will receive a share of the revenues (Bloomsbury 2011).

All other Bloomsbury response options are aimed at the trade and not the consumer (Figure 4.30).

4.3.5.5 Frontlist E-marketing

Kelman's book *Pigeon English* is listed on Bloomsbury's main page, with a hint to its shortlisting for the Man Booker Prize 2011 (Figure 4.31). When clicking on the picture, the reader gets to the dedicated webpage (www.pigeonenglish.co.uk) with more information on book and author; there is also the trailer video and author interviews and downloadable reading group information. The author has no Facebook or Twitter accounts and no blog; there are no links to share the information on social media either.

4.3.5.6 Summary Bloomsbury

Bloomsbury's website has a good mixture of content for consumers and trade customers, offering targeted content and implemented prize information where possible. Bloomsbury could profit, however, from more social media exposure of their authors and a closer tie-in of used platforms, such as in the case of Pottermore, which is fully linked and tied-in, even though Rowling set it up without Bloomsbury's involvement.

Figure 4.24 Bloomsbury Main Webpage

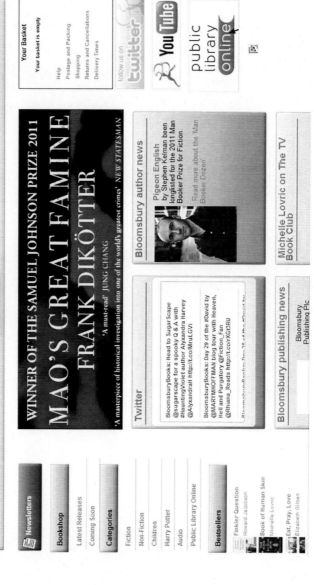

Figure 4.25 Bloomsbury Additional Information

Figure 4.26 Bloomsbury Children's Books

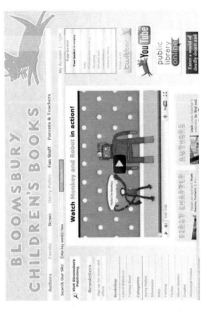

Figure 4.27 Bloomsbury Harry Potter

Figure 4.28 Bloomsbury Social Media Links

Figure 4.29 Bloomsbury Sharing on Social Media

Figure 4.30 Bloomsbury Contact Us

Copyright enquiries
Harry Potter rights and copyright enquiries
Sales enquiries from bookstores within the UK
Sales enquiries from bookstores outside the UK and US
UK catalogue requests
US catalog requests
Press enquiries
Children's publicity enquiries
Reference Enquiries
All other enquiries

Figure 4.31 Bloomsbury Frontlist Title

4.3.6 Portobello Books

4.3.6.1 Publisher Profile

London-based Portobello Books (Portobello) was founded in 2005 and came out with four books that year. In 2006, they acquired Granta Books and merged the two companies. They since share design, sales, marketing, publicity, rights and production. With 21 employees, Portobello now has a focus on non-fiction books, and was shortlisted for the Independent Publisher of the Year Award in 2009 (Portobello 2011). Portobello publishes internationalist literature and activist non-fiction (Herbert 2010, p. 178).

4.3.6.2 Website

Portobello's website has information on their books (*Explore Portobello Books*), the company history (*About Portobello Books*), employment, contact information, the Granta Magazine and Granta Books (Figure 4.32). The *Explore Portobello Books* section offers the newest titles categorized by the publication month up to six months in advance and a selection of the six essential Portobello titles for the interested reader. There is also a list of Portobello authors and a search function; however, there is no comprehensive list of Portobello titles.

Events where readers can meet Portobello authors in person are listed under the *About Portobello Books* section, which is not necessarily intuitive.

The website does not have an integrated online shop; the consumer is offered links to buy online via Amazon and Waterstone's.

4.3.6.3 Social Media

Portobello does not invite the consumer to join or follow Portobello on social media anywhere on the website. Portobello has no Facebook presence and no Twitter account; Granta, however, does have a Twitter account.

4.3.6.4 Consumer Response

Consumers will find it difficult to contact Portobello. A general email is in the *Contact Us* section, but apart from that, Portobello offers no consumer response forum.

All other options to contact Portobello are aimed at the trade and media, or those seeking employment with Portobello (Figure 4.33).

4.3.6.5 Frontlist E-marketing

The publisher's website contains a dedicated page for Birnbaum's book *Season to Taste* with information on the author and the book. This dedicated webpage contains no links to the author's presence on social media or to her blog, which comes up with an Internet search at www.mollysmadeleinerecipes.blogspot.com/. The author writes about her experiences and posts recipes on this blog. She also has a user page on Facebook; it is not clear whether she accepts friend requests from fans on this page. She does have a Twitter account and just over 300 followers.

4.3.6.6 Summary Portobello

Portobello seemingly markets primarily to the trade; they make no visible concerted effort to integrate B2C e-marketing tools and techniques.

Figure 4.33 Working With Portobello

Figure 4.32 Portobello Books Main Webpage

4.3.7 Canongate

4.3.7.1 Company Profile

Canongate is an Edinburgh-based publisher of general non-fiction and fiction (Herbert 2010, p. 145). They had a growth rate of over 300% in 2009 (Neilan 2009). Founded in 1973, Jamie Byng bought Canongate in 1994 when they had financial problems; Byng still manages Canongate. In 2003 and again in 2009, Canongate was awarded the Publisher of the Year Award for their "great professionalism, attention to detail and sheer exuberance of [their] publishing programme" (Myers 2009).

4.3.7.2 Website

Canongate's website changed significantly during the course of this research (Figure 4.34 and Figure 4.35). As stated on the old website, Canongate's web presence is atypical. The website is in the domain *.tv*, normally reserved for the Pacific island of Tuvalu; this makes visitors think of the abbreviation for television. Canongate aims to bring together ("channel") all information and media about their books and authors on their website (Canongate 2011). The visitor can either navigate the website via the navigation bar or click on the channels featured on the main page (Figure 4.35).

4.3.7.3 Social Media

Canongate invites the visitor on their main page to connect on Facebook, Twitter, and YouTube (Figure 4.38). On dedicated book webpages, they provide buttons to share information on social media (Figure 4.39). When following an author or book onto the respective "channel", there are no further links to connect with either on social media, just links to share the information with friends.

4.3.7.4 Consumer Response

Canongate invites their readers to log in to the site and tell Canongate about their interests. Creating an account takes only a few minutes; once the account is set up, the visitor can order directly from Canongate and create book reviews on the page. Canongate is very responsive to their followers on Twitter and Facebook; only very few posts and questions remain unanswered.

Canongate provides a contact form for consumers and trade, inducing comments and enquiries. On the *Introducing Canongate.tv* channel, they invite visitors to "tell us what you are interested in at Canongate", but at the time of research, there is no forum for the interested reader to actually do that yet (Figure 4.36).

4.3.7.5 Frontlist E-marketing

Canongate has created a platform on which they bring together all information available on their authors and books. The channel of the frontlist author, Walsh, hosts an array of information: a video on the author's motivation for writing *Go to Sleep*, her website, links to other related websites, interviews with Walsh, and reviews by bloggers and newspapers. However, there are no links to the authors' social media presence on the publisher's site or her linked website; the author's and her literary agent's email address are the only ways to contact her.

4.3.7.6 Summary Canongate

Canongate underwent a recent change in their online presence, trying to capitalize on their new *.tv* domain and providing their consumers with channels bringing together relevant information. Canongate engages with their consumers well on social media but could probably profit from tying-in their authors more closely and establishing brand awareness.

Figure 4.34 Old Canongate Main Page

Figure 4.35 New Main Webpage Canongate

Figure 4.36 Canongate Reader Account

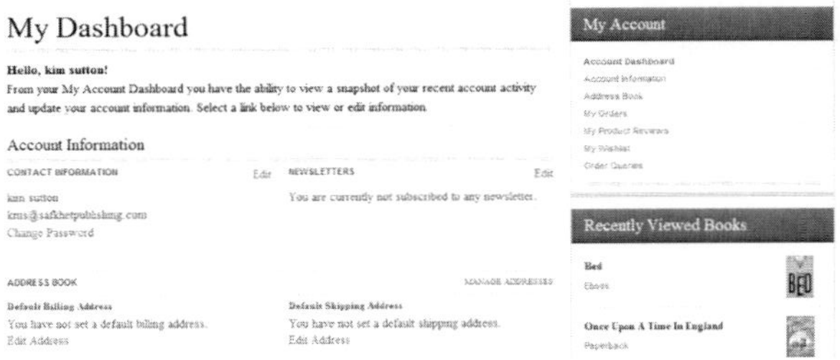

Figure 4.37 Canongate Link to Community

Figure 4.38 Canongate Social Media Invitation

Figure 4.39 Canongate Social Media Sharing

4.4 Cross-Case Summary

4.4.1 Overview

This research examines publishers' B2C e-marketing efforts with a focus on UK-based trade publishers and the specific tools and forums they use, summarized in Table 4.2. Individual aspects are described in the previous sections for each case study.

Table 4.2 Publishers' B2C Efforts

Publisher	Salt	Nosy Crow	PS	Gollancz	Bloomsbury	Portobello	Canongate
website							
navigation bar	X	X	X	X	X	X	X
news	X	X	X	X	X	X	X
visitors invited to share on social networks	X	-	-	-	-	-	-
embedded publisher's blog	-	X	-	-	-	-	X
external publisher's blog	X	-	X	X	-	-	-
RSS feed available	X	X	X	X	-	-	-
links to author blogs	X	-	-	X	X	X	X
online shop	X	-	X	-	X	-	X
reviews	-	X	X	-	-	-	X
events	-	X	-	X	X	X	X
prizes	X	-	-	X	-	-	X
information for reading groups	-	-	-	X	X	-	-
social media							
visitors invited to follow on							
Facebook	X	X	X	-	-	-	X
Twitter	X	X	X	-	X	-	X
YouTube	X	X	X	-	X	-	X
cross-promoted content	-	X	-	-	X	-	X
embedded videos	X	X	-	-	X	-	X
interactive games	-	-	-	-	X	-	X
consumer response							
recommendation form for new author/book	X	-	-	-	-	-	-
contact form/information	X	X	-	-	X	-	X
contact information without a form	-	-	X	X	-	X	-
Stage according to Bernoff	*II*	*III*	*II*	*II*	*III*	*II*	*IV*

[source and categorization: Sutton 2011, compiled during August 2011]

Bernoff (2011 and June 2011), as mentioned in the literature critique, categorizes companies' managing of social technology into five stages: dormant (I), testing (II), coordinating (III), scaling and optimizing (IV), and empowered (V) (compare 2.5). Based on the findings described in section 4.3 and the respective summaries, publishers are categorized using Bernoff's five stages, as shown in the last line in Table 4.2. All researched publishers are actively e-marketing their books, but to varying degrees. More than half of the researched publishers are testing, two are coordinating, and one is scaling and optimizing, according to Bernoff. Although this is not statistically relevant, it does show that within the research, most publishers are not fully using the Internet and modern e-marketing tools to their advantage.

The following sections summarize the findings of the case studies, grouped by website, e-marketing, social media, consumer response, and frontlist e-marketing.

4.4.2 Website

The publishers designed their websites very differently with recurring features. All publishers have a navigation bar in addition to other linking features on their website, and they all post news about themselves. Only Salt invites visitors to share their main website on social media. Canongate provides a blog but no RSS feed for the reader. This may be due to the current restructuring of Canongate's website. Four publishers link to their authors' blogs; some authors do not seem to write blogs at all, while others' blogs are not cross-promoted on the publishers' websites.

The publishers who do not offer an online shop have links on the book pages that send visitors to e-tailer platforms such as Amazon, Waterstone's and play.com for a convenient shopping experience.

The researched publishers have very different additional information on their sites: two link to or post book reviews, four post information on author and book events, two have information on prizes that their books have won or were short or long listed for, and two provide reading group guides. Canongate found a very intuitive system to bundle all information related to a book or author into their channels, so that the website visitors find all information in one convenient location. All other publishers group the information by category (news, events, prizes, et cetera).

4.4.3 Social Media

Only half of the publishers are inviting their readers to follow them on Facebook, one more has included invitations to follow on Twitter and YouTube. Only two publishers cross-promote content between their main website, social media accounts, blogs, and other related sites. Three offer embedded videos for the visitor to watch and two have linked games.

Table 4.3 Statistics for Publishers on Social Networking Sites

Publisher	Salt	Nosy Crow	PS	Gollancz	Bloomsbury	Portobello	Canongate
Twitter followers	30,951	3,987	279	3,470	15,969	-	8,063
Following on Twitter	30,354	945	46	502	1,316	-	215
Listed on Twitter	1,868	251	19	368	1,176	-	585
Facebook fans	886	842	98	1,967+3,720	-	1	1,681
Ratio followers/ following	1.02	4.21	6.06	6.91	12.13	-	37.50

[source: Sutton 2011, compiled during August 2011]

Table 4.3 shows that not all publishers are active on social media sites. The numbers of followers on Twitter are possibly deceptive. Salt is following only a few users less than are actively following Salt. Twitter actually calls this practice "aggressive following" (Twitter Help 2011) and rightfully so points out that it is highly unlikely that a user like Salt would actually be able to keep up with updates from over 30,000 users they follow themselves. Despite their numbers of followers being quite high, it is thus safe to assume that Salt's followers simply follow them right back rather than actually being interested in Salt's content.

The ratio of followers/following in the last line of Table 4.3 means that the publisher has so many people following them for every one user they follow. Canongate has, by far, the best and most impressive ratio with 37.5 followers per person they follow; Bloomsbury also has a good ratio, although it is again doubtful that they keep up with over 1,300 users and their individual tweets.

The numbers of Facebook fans speak for the fact that none of the publishers is making sophisticated use of Facebook yet; for comparison: Simon & Schuster has 19,068 fans, Penguin Books 25,839, and Random House 18,977 (Facebook 2011).

4.4.4 Consumer Response

There is varied evidence of the publishers actively seeking consumer response and integrating the consumer's wishes.

Salt invites their readers to submit book recommendations for publication. Three publishers have contact forms so the visitor can send their enquiries via the publishers' websites. The other three have contact information such as email addresses and phone numbers without a specific form for the consumer. There is no evidence of how the publishers react to consumer enquiries. There is no further consumer response invited on the websites; no publisher uses Facebook's social plugins, with which consumers could respond directly on the publisher's website making the website automatically appear in the consumer's Facebook profile.

4.4.5 Frontlist E-marketing

One book from each publisher was followed to investigate whether the author makes an extra effort beyond the publisher's e-marketing endeavors.

Table 4.4 shows that only four of the publishers invite their readers to share the frontlist books on social media. While it is possibly negligible that consumers share the publisher's general website with their friends and followers, it is careless not to provide easy means for sharing the (frontlist) books. No convenient tool is available if a reader wants to share the information; he must manually share it using other methods.

All publishers have easy-to-find, dedicated webpages for their books. Nosy Crow and Bloomsbury have external, linked pages with individual URLs (www.smallbluething.com; www.pigeonenglish.co.uk). The authors for the PS and Portobello frontlist books both have blogs that the publisher does not link to; the interested reader has to find these via a search engine or other method.

Three of the publishers post the book trailer for the respective book on their website; the trailers are all hosted by YouTube.

Table 4.4 Publishers' Frontlist E-marketing

One book of Publisher's Frontlist	Salt	Nosy Crow	PS	Gollancz	Bloomsbury	Portobello	Canongate
Reader invited to share on social media	X	-	X	X	-	-	X
Dedicated webpage for the book	X	X	X	X	X	X	X
External book page with individual URL	-	X	-	-	X	-	-
Author blog	-	-	X	X	-	X	X
Author fans on Facebook page	-	36	-	-	-	-	-
Author Twitter followers	-	280	-	1326	-	364	-
Author/ book page linked on publisher page	-	X	-	X	X	-	X
Newsletter	-	X	-	-	-	-	-
Video Trailer	-	X	-	-	X	-	X

[source: Sutton 2011, compiled during August 2011]

4.5 Conclusion

This chapter proffered an introduction on the publishers, the individual detailed descriptions of the case studies, and a cross-case summary. The case studies showed that the diverse websites make use of different techniques, tools, and themes. All publishers offer either online shops or links to other e-tailers like Amazon, while only four publishers invite their readers to follow them on social networking sites, and only two cross-promote their author's Internet content.

The cross-case summary confirms that most publishers are in the testing or coordinating stages of managing social technology for marketing purposes; only Canongate is in stage IV: *scaling and optimizing*, categorized according to Bernoff. Portobello was categorized as being in the *testing* phase only due to their authors' presences on social media, otherwise their categorization would have been *dormant*. None of the researched publishers has a significant following on social networking sites while having a decent follower/following ratio.

Chapter 5 discusses the findings of the case studies.

5 Discussion of the Findings

5.1 Introduction

The focus of this research is on UK publishers' transition from B2B to B2C marketers and, more specifically, their current efforts in B2C e-marketing. While the previous chapter described publishers' efforts, this chapter draws links back to the literature critique from chapter 2 and discusses publisher's e-marketing efforts. Section 5.2 offers links to literature and an opinionated discussion of the findings; section 5.3 shows and explains the revised model in Figure 5.1, and section 5.4 offers a conclusion.

5.2 Findings

5.2.1 Overview

Table 5.1 gives an overview on the links of the research findings back to the literature discussed in chapter 2. Each factor is discussed in turn.

Table 5.1 Findings Linked to Literature

Website	link to literature
Product-driven marketing	change shoppers into buyers; single-step buying process (Morva 2005); rise of e-tailers (Thompson 2005)
Marketing planning	consistent marketing plans and communication with consumers (Solomon, Marshall and Stuart 2006; Borges 2009); publishers control over 4 Ps (Clark 2008)
360-degree marketing	employ every method possible; constant online brand recall (Blackwell 2006); connect with consumer (Clark 2008; Borges 2009; Aaker 2011; Zarrella 2011; O'Reilly 2005); added value (Hollensen 2004)
Fast-paced technology	new and quickly changing methods (Solomon, Marshall and Stuart 2006; Thompson 2005); growing e-marketing (Kotler 2010);
Viral marketing	get customers to talk (Kotler 2010; Clark and Phillips 2008; Zarella 2011)
Trendsetting	publisher as trendsetter, not direct sales person (Shatzkin 2010)

[source: Sutton 2011]

5.2.2 Product-Driven Marketing

According to Morva (2005), consumer marketing is product-driven and ultimately aimed at turning a shopper into a buyer by offering convincing sales arguments and a convenient shopping experience. The research has shown that not all publishers provide the consumer with product-driven marketing and a single-step buying platform; some link to external providers.

When following amazon.co.uk from the Gollancz webpage, a new window opens for Amazon, in which the consumer has to click on the item again, log into Amazon and continue shopping from there. Gollancz and Nosy Crow risk that the consumer does not return to their page to continue shopping; Portobello is even more at risk of losing the consumer, as Amazon opens in the same window, forcing the consumer to go back and forth in the browser. On the other hand, publishers who do sell their books via Amazon make themselves discoverable by Amazon shoppers who have not heard of the publisher and just follow the internal Amazon recommendation system, or those who are already loyal Amazon customers.

5.2.3 Marketing Planning

Solomon et al. (2006) point out the importance of marketing planning and communicating a consistent message to the consumer. It is not possible to deduce the publishers' individual marketing strategies. However, by comparing the cross-case findings to the frontlist marketing findings (Table 4.4), it becomes evident that not all publishers communicate the same message as their authors, not all authors are active on online platforms at all, and their respective online content is not cross-promoted. PS' frontlist author Jack Dann, for example, has a blog linking to PS, while PS, in turn, does not link to this blog on their webpage. PS does not use all possible methods to present the consumer with a consistent image and all available information.

It is perfunctory of publishers not to take control of the entire marketing mix where they can; as described in section 2.4.1, they could have much more control when marketing (and thus selling) directly to the consumer. Careful consideration is necessary when deciding to sell via Amazon, and thus giving up a part of the margin, while possibly driving the consumer away from the publisher's website; the advantage of integration into Amazon's bestseller lists and recommendation program might outweigh the margin cut.

5.2.4 360-Degree Marketing

Blackwell (2006) points out the importance of e-marketing to reach the consumer while offering constant brand recall. It is surprising to see that Gollancz and Portobello do not market on social media platforms; they are not present where some potential consumers are. Even more astonishing is that not all publishers provide the consumer with a means to connect to them, and that very few publishers offer any added value, such as reading group notes or games (Hollensen 2004). Canongate is the only publisher that links to a related community on the Internet (Figure 4.37). To follow literature's consensus, a more ambitious movement would be for publishers to engage and integrate the readers on platforms such as HarperCollins' *authonomy* in order to utilize, implement, and realize the readers' requests.

5.2.5 Fast-paced Technology

There is a general consensus in literature that new and fast-paced technologies bring forward challenges and opportunities to companies and consumers. Communication takes place instantaneously without country boundaries, and companies who do not partake in this are disadvantaged and risk business (Solomon, Marshall and Stuart 2006; Kotler and Armstrong 2010; Newlands 2011; Thompson 2005; Kotler 2011). Considering this, it is curious that there are established publishers (Gollancz) who do not partake in modern technology; this may be because they are, in fact, traditional companies and might find it difficult to adapt.

5.2.6 Viral Marketing

Kotler (2010) points out the need to increase online marketing activity so that consumers talk about products on the Internet. Clark and Phillips (2008) and Zarella (2011) point out that the Internet and social websites are opportune places to foster consumer relationships and start "contagious campaigns". Only Canongate is on the way to full integration with social media. This dichotomy is not reasonable, as most social media sites provide social plugins for website developers to integrate on their own website; utilizing these tools is easy, fast, and free. Publishers who do not make use of these tools neglect to follow the trend and ignore that many people spend a lot of time online talking to their friends and relations, and sharing information as well as recommendations.

5.2.7 Trendsetting

Not all publishers follow the general trend of social media participation; the only publisher found to be actually setting trends and addressing consumers in a non-selling fashion among the researched publishers is Canongate. Canongate's new website focuses on providing information and a good experience for the reader while providing easy, one-stop buying opportunities. They are the only publisher that scales and optimizes, and thus is in Bernoff's (2011) stage IV. Their new website is trendsetting, as it is consumer-oriented and focused on providing information; it remains to be seen whether Canongate implements more consumer-feedback-related technology.

Salt, having managed to raise enough funds to stay in business with their online campaign "Just One Book" (Salt 2011; Bookseller 2009), is also a trendsetter.

5.3 Implications and Revision to the Model

Implementing the findings of the case studies, the author modified the model, as shown in Figure 5.1.

The aspect **publisher** was adjusted to encompass or incorporate all other aspects. The publisher should be the controlling organ around all efforts to market a content provider's work, and steer the marketing, while at the same time allowing the content provider to build platforms and form relationships with his readers. The publisher should also create platforms for the content provider and foster relationships with consumers, providing as much relevant information in appropriate places as possible.

Figure 5.1 Publishers' B2C Activities (Adjusted Model)

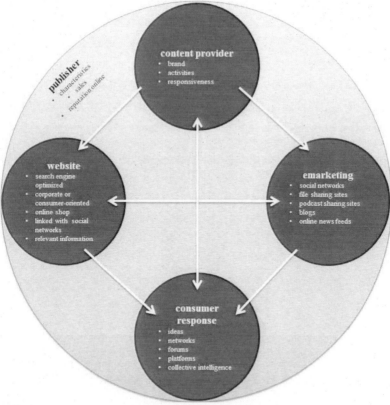

[source: Sutton 2011]

5.4 Conclusion

This chapter discusses the case study research on publishers' B2C e-marketing efforts. The tools and forums in use by the researched publishers are linked back to existing literature.

The originality of this research is its focus on UK trade publishers and their e-marketing related activities. To the author's knowledge, there has been no other research to date specifically focused on publishers' B2C e-marketing activities.

The findings underline the importance of publishers' modern e-marketing activities in order to reach the consumer and provide them with relevant information. Prior to B2C e-marketing, publishers barely had the chance to implement direct feedback and participate as a proactive, modern, and trend-creating publisher. They can now become product-driven and concentrate on developing channels to consumers. Planning and coordinating marketing efforts remain ever important and should include e-marketing, possibly involving specialists with technological expertise. A modern marketing campaign cannot ignore e-marketing and possibilities on the Internet; publishers, in particular, should be adapting quicker to publishing content in fast-paced technological environments. Publishers who manage this will be able to foster relationships with individual consumers, ignite viral campaigns, and set trends for their own future.

Chapter 6 concludes this discussion by outlining the contributions to knowledge, identifying possibilities for future research, and providing an overall conclusion of this research.

6 Conclusions and Recommendations for Further Research

6.1 Introduction

Chapter 5 discusses the analysis of the case studies on publishers' B2C marketing in light of existing literature. Chapter 6 builds on those findings by highlighting their contribution to knowledge (6.2) and limitations (6.3), identifying points for future research (6.4), and completing this dissertation with overall conclusions (6.5).

6.2 Contribution to Knowledge and Recommendations

This dissertation contributes to better understanding publishers' e-marketing efforts, and offers a model by which publishers can assess their B2C e-marketing.

6.2.1 How can publishers transition from B2B to B2C marketing (Q1)?

It is important to understand *success* before addressing a successful transition from B2B to B2C marketing. In this context, success is the publishers' gaining of loyal consumers resulting in full control over the marketing mix and an increase of the publishers' bottom line.

Publishers can reach this by focusing on product-driven marketing, and making consumers aware of their products (books and authors) on regularly visited platforms. While still fostering partnerships with the trade, publishers should continue to build relationships with individual consumers and consumer groups.

Sections 6.2.2 and 6.2.3 describe in detail how publishers can use social media and their websites to reach individual consumers.

6.2.2 How can publishers make use of social media (Q2)?

When considering fast-paced technology and adapting to new trends quickly, publishers can integrate social media marketing in their marketing planning and core business. A publisher who is poorly represented on social media may lose business by being non-traceable to certain consumers. Being active on social media is a publisher's chance to spark viral campaigns and connect to the consumer, while giving him a chance to shape the community and contribute his experience and wishes. Following Bernoff's stages would be a good starting point for publishers to master social evolution. Publishers would do well in hosting blogs and integrating the information into all social media platforms they use with social technology, so that blog content feeds automatically into connected social media accounts.

6.2.3 How can publishers set up their websites to interest more consumers (Q3)?

Publishers who include the consumers' needs in their research and conclusively shape their websites can attract more readers, as they deliver exactly the content readers want. To achieve this, publishers should start by being present on all relevant platforms; they should be accessible, be available, and listen to their readers, while observing and embracing customers' ideas. Publishers or editors can participate in numerous forums in order to engage with consumers and find out what currently interests them on the Internet; these forums vary depending on the subject of the book. Most authors will know the relevant forums and publishers should integrate them by linking to them and supporting the author's presence on those forums and platforms.

6.2.4 What can publishers learn from other companies' transition to a B2C marketing approach (Q4)?

The scope of this research did not allow for an answer to this question. More research is necessary to answer it; an industry would have to first be identified that did in fact make a successful transition from B2B to B2C.

6.3 Limitations

The author acknowledges the limitations of her conclusions, namely the study's use of a small, non-representative sample and the fact that this does not allow for generalization. This limitation is a direct result of the chosen methodology: qualitative research with multiple in-depth case studies. Qualitative research was chosen to be most appropriate to understand the research questions, as they are of a *how* and *why* nature; this research does not seek to generalize, but rather to reach theoretical conclusions. These limitations are common in case study research (Hollensen 2004).

A further limitation is that the research focuses on only one country, namely the UK. This needs to be kept in mind when examining the study's findings, as cultural differences may play a role when publishers start to implement B2C e-marketing.

6.4 Implications for Further Research

Future research on publishers' B2C e-marketing activities could test these findings on a larger scale. By making the research consumer-based, the focus could be placed on the consumers' perception of publishers, content providers and books as brands, and what type of e-marketing the consumer sees as necessary, appealing, and relevant. Quantitative research would allow for the generalization of the findings with statistical testing.

Further research is also needed on the research question 4, as mentioned in 6.2.4.

Another interesting aspect not covered by this research is publishers' perceptions of what is necessary and actually implemented for consumer-based marketing. In-depth qualitative case studies with publishers who have already implemented B2C e-marketing, such as Canongate and Salt, would be informative and insightful.

6.5 Conclusion

This research brings together literature on the publishing industry and on modern marketing, and e-marketing in particular. It draws on the author's experience with websites and social media, as well as business (development) and her degree in publishing, and investigates the efforts of modern publishers in a transition from B2B marketers to B2C e-marketers. In doing so, it advances knowledge on the topic, in particular on publishers' current B2C e-marketing endeavors.

The literature critique shows that publishers should bring relevant content and information on their products to their online consumers, embrace modern technology, and become active on social media and the Web 2.0. This would allow them to interact with their readers and implement gained impetus, resulting in full control over their marketing mix. Consumers would talk about their products on modern platforms. Publishers could then increase sales and gain brand awareness for their own brand, as well as author and book brands.

The model designed for the case studies was revised afterwards to reflect the encompassing function of the publisher. With this model, publishers' e-marketing efforts can be investigated and categorized. Particularly together with Bernoff's stages, it is then possible to classify publishers and their managing of social technology.

The seven case studies show that publishers are using very different tools, techniques, and themes for their e-marketing; most of them are in the testing or coordinating stages of using social media for marketing purposes, only one of them is scaling and optimizing. Publishers need to reach modern consumers and should utilize the Internet and social media for this. Well-planned, product-driven e-marketing becomes more important as publishers need to create and foster lasting relationships with individuals in order to turn them into loyal customers.

This dissertation identified six factors that play a vital role in B2C e-marketing. First, B2C e-marketing should be **product-driven**. Marketing activities should be consistently **planned** and carried out accordingly. Modern **360-degree marketing** needs to incorporate all available platforms, including relevant forums and social media. Publishers should follow the **fast-paced technology**, particularly if they want to spark and follow **viral campaigns**. Publishers who follow these key findings throughout their B2C e-marketing efforts are indeed seen as **trendsetting**. The best-practice example identified by this research is Canongate.

These insights set a foundation for further research on publishers' B2C e-marketing activities, and thus their transition from a traditionally B2B industry to a modern B2C industry.

References

Aaker, D., July 30, 2001. Beyond Communication to Changing the Marketplace. *Marketing News*. [Online] Available at <http://www.marketingpower.com/ResourceLibrary/Publications/MarketingNews/2011/7-30-11/aaker.pdf> [Accessed August 2011].

authonomy, 2011. *authonomy writing community*. [Online] Available at <http://www.authonomy.com> [Accessed August 2011].

Baverstock, A., 1997. *How to Market Books*. Second edition. London: Kogan Page.

Baverstock, A., Bowen, S. and Carey, S., 2008. *How to Get a Job in Publishing*. London: A & C Black Publishers Ltd.

Bernoff, J., July 30, 2011. Corporate Social Evolution. *Marketing News*. [Online] Available at <http://www.marketingpower.com/ResourceLibrary/Publications/MarketingNews/2011/7-30-11/social%20media.pdf> [Accessed August 2011].

Bernoff, J., June 3, 2011. Managing Social Technology by Stages. *Harvard Business Review*. [Blog] Available at: <http://blogs.hbr.org/cs/2011/06/managing_social_technology_by.html> [Accessed August 2011].

Bickers, J., February 16, 2007. The Young and the Graphic Novel. *Publishers Weekly*. [Online] Available at: <http://www.publishersweekly.com/pw/by-topic/new-titles/adult-announcements/article/4884-the-young-and-the-graphic-novel-.html> [Accessed July 20, 2011].

Birnbaum, M., July 16, 2011. Tabasco with Everything. *The Guardian Weekend*, pp. 17-21.

Blackwell, J., 2006. *Overview of Traditional Marketing*. [Online] Available at <http://ezinearticles.com/?Overview-of-Traditional-Marketing&id=374128> [Accessed July 22, 2011].

Bloomsbury, 2011. *Bloomsbury*. [Online] Available at: <www.bloomsbury.com> [Accessed July and August 2011].

Bookseller, 2009. Indie Salt Shakes Off Closure Threat. *Bookseller*, 5393, p. 8. [Online] Business Source Premier, EBSCOhost [Accessed August 3, 2011].

Borges, B., 2009. *Marketing 2.0: Bridging the Gap between Seller and Buyer through Social Media Marketing*. Tucson: Wheatmark.

Campbell, L., June 1, 2011a. Gardners' Hive Launches with 350 Indies on Board. *Bookseller*. [Online] Available at <http://www.thebookseller.com/news/gardners-hive-launches-350-indies-board.html> [Accessed July and August 2011].

Campbell, L., June 15, 2011b. Sandwich Bookshop to Close. *Bookseller*. [Online] Available at <http://www.thebookseller.com/news/sandwich-bookshop-close.html> [Accessed September 2011].

Campbell, L., August 24, 2011c. High Street "A Goner" Says Cumbrian Indie Owner. *Bookseller*. [Online] Available at <http://www.thebookseller.com/news/high-street-goner-says-cumbrian-indie-owner.html> [Accessed September 2011].

Canongate Books, 2011. *Meet at the Gate - Home*. [Online] Available at: <http://www.canongate.net/> [Accessed July and August 2011].

Clark, G. and Phillips, A., 2008. *Inside Book Publishing*. Abingdon: Routledge.

Davies, I., July 4, 2005. Talis, Web 2.0 and All That. *Internet Alchemy*. [Blog] Available at <http://blog.iandavis.com/2005/07/04/talis-web-2-0-and-all-that/> [Accessed September 2011].

de Bertodano, H., July 16, 2011. My Life in Heels, Skirts and Lip Gloss. *The Times Magazine*, pp. 38-42.

Denscombe, M., 2007. *The Good Research Guide*. Third Edition. Berkshire: Open University Press; McGraw-Hill Education.

Ephron, H., 2011. *The Everything Guide to Writing Your First Novel*. Avon: Adams Media.

Facebook, 2011. *Welcome to Facebook*. [Online] Available at: <http://www.facebook.com/> [Accessed July and August 2011].

Gollancz 2011. *SF & Fantasy – Orion Books*. [Online] Available at <http://www.orionbooks.co.uk/genres/sf-fantasy> [Accessed July and August 2011].

Flood, A., June 23, 2011. Pottermore Website Launched by JK Rowling as 'Give-Back' to Fans. *guardian.co.uk*. [Online] Available at <http://www.guardian.co.uk/books/2011/jun/23/pottermore-website-jk-rowling-harry-potter> [Accessed August 5, 2011].

Gardner, R., June 30, 2011. Do Publishers Market Books? *Rachelle Gardner*. [Blog] Available at <http://www.rachellegardner.com/2011/06/do-publishers-market-books/> [Accessed August 19, 2011].

Gardner, R., August 2, 2011. How to Market Your Book. *Rachelle Gardner*. [Blog] Available at <http://www.rachellegardner.com/2011/08/how-to-market-your-book/> [Accessed August 19, 2011].

Gardner, R., August 16, 2011. Will Self-Pub Sales Affect Your Future? *Rachelle Gardner*. [Blog] Available at <http://www.rachellegardner.com/2011/06/do-publishers-market-books/> [Accessed August 19, 2011].

Gunelius, S., 2011. *30-Minute Social Media Marketing*. [e-book]. New York: McGraw-Hill. Available through Google Books <http://books.google.com/books?id=8jRTUB0nI9IC&printsec=frontcover#v=onepage&q=f=false> [Accessed July 18, 2011].

Hall, J., September 2, 2011. Internet and Supermarkets Kill off 2,000 Bookshops. *The Telegraph*. [Online] Available at <http://www.telegraph.co.uk/culture/books/booknews/8738701/Internet-and-supermarkets-kill-off-2000-bookshops.html> [Accessed September 2011].

Herbert, J., 2010. *Writers' & Artists' Yearbook 2011*. London: A&C Black.

Hollensen, S., 2004. *Global Marketing*. Harlow: Pearson Education Limited.

Horn, C., 2010. Wilson Founds Nosy Start-Up. *Bookseller*, 5421, p. 10. [Online] Business Source Premier, EBSCOhost. [Accessed August 3, 2011].

Hyatt, M., June 28, 2011. Four Reasons Why You Must Take Responsibility for Your Own Marketing. *MH Michael Hyatt Intentional Leadership*. [Blog] Available at <http://michaelhyatt.com/four-reasons-why-you-must-take-responsibility-for-your-own-marketing.html> [Accessed August 19, 2011].

Kalder, D., September 19, 2011. Ready Reader One: Why Gamification is Key to Publishing's Future. *Publishing Perspectives – International Publishing News and Opinion*. [Online] Available at <http://publishingperspectives.com/2011/09/gamification-key-publishing-future/> [Accessed September 2011].

Kotler, P. 2011. Reinventing Marketing to Manage the Environmental Imperative. *Journal of Marketing*. American Marketing Association: Volume 75, Number 4.

Kotler, P. and Armstrong, G., 2010. *Principles of Marketing*. Upper Saddle River: Pearson Prentice Hall.

Kremer, J., 1998. *1001 Ways to Market Your Book*. Fairfield: Open Horizons.

Miller, M., March 8, 2011. Study: LinkedIn is More Effective for B2B Companies. *HubSpot Blog*. [Blog] Available at <http://blog.hubspot.com/blog/tabid/6307/bid/10437/Study-LinkedIn-Is-More-Effective-for-B2B-Companies.aspx> [Accessed August 2011].

Morva, T., April 8, 2009. B2B versus B2C Marketing. *Ezine Articles*. [Online] Available at <http://ezinearticles.com/?B2B-Versus-B2C-Marketing&id=407950> [Accessed July and August 2011].

Myers, B., June 3, 3009. Canongate: Making Passion and Daring Pay. *Guardian Books Blog*. [Blog] Available at <http://www.guardian.co.uk/books/booksblog/2009/jun/03/canongate-passion-daring-pay> [Accessed August 25, 2011].

Neilan, C., May 31, 2009. Indie Alliance Publishers Grow Sales 60%. *Bookseller*. [Online] Available at <http://www.thebookseller.com/news/indie-alliance-publishers-grow-sales-60.html?quicktabs_1=1> [Accessed July and August 2011].

Neill, G, March 2, 2011. Waterstone's Parent Buys Stake in 'Social Bookselling' Website. *Bookseller*. [Online] Available at <http://www.thebookseller.com/news/waterstones-parent-buys-stake-social-bookselling-website.html> [Accessed July and August 2011].

Newlands, M., 2011. *Online Marketing. A User's Manual*. Hoboken: Jon Wiley & Sons.

Nosy Crow, 2011. *Welcome :: Nosy Crow*. [Online] Available at <http://www.nosycrow.com> [Accessed July and August 2011].

O'Reilly, T., September 30, 2005. What is Web 2.0 Design Patterns and Business Models for the Next Generation of Software. *O'Reilly*. [Blog] Available at <http://oreilly.com/web2/archive/what-is-web-20.html> [Accessed August 20, 2011].

Odyl, 2011. *Odyl | Odyl Helps Authors and Publishers Connect With Readers on Facebook*. [Online] Available at <http://odyl.net/> [Accessed September 2011].

Pallot, W., 2011. *Corporate and Investor Relations – Financial Results*. [Online] Available at <http://www.bloomsbury-ir.co.uk/html/financial/f_latest.html#chair> [Accessed July and August 2011].

Portobello Books, 2011. *Portobello Books*. [Online] Available at: <http://www.portobellobooks.com/> [Accessed July and August 2011].

Pride, W.M. and Ferrell, O.C., 2010. *Marketing*. Sixteenth edition. Mason: South-Western Cengage Learning.

PS Publishing, 2011. *UK Genre Publishing of SF, Horror & Fantasy Fiction*. [Online] Available at: <http://www.pspublishing.co.uk/> [Accessed July and August 2011].

Ranchhod, A., 2004. *Marketing Strategies – A Twenty-First Century Approach*. Harlow: Pearson Education Limited.

Reed, J., 2010. Small and Mighty. *Publishing Talk. Mashing up Books and Social Media*. [Online] Available at <http://www.publishingtalk.eu/featured/small-and-mighty/> [Accessed July and August 2011].

Richardson, P., 2008. *The UK Publishing Industry*. London: The Publishers Association.

Roberts, C., May 19, 2011. Mums Nuns and Warrington. *Roberts*. [Blog] Available at <http://imedia.brookes.ac.uk/roberts/entry/mums_nuns_and_warrington/> [Accessed July and August 2011].

Ronai, F., November 13, 2009. Digital Focus: Word of Mouth. *The Bookseller*. [Online] Available at <http://www.thebookseller.com/feature/digital-focus-word-mouth.html> [Accessed July and August 2011].

Rowling, J.K., 2011. Follow the Owl to Pottermore. [Video Online] Available at <http://harrypotter.bloomsbury.com/video> [Accessed August 5, 2011].

Salt Publishing, 2011. International Award-Winning Poetry and Short Story Publishers. [Online] Available at: <http://saltpublishing.com/> [Accessed July and August 2011].

Sayce, K., July 20, 2011. Direct-to-Consumer – It's the Way to Go. *Blogs | FutureBook*. [Online] Available at <http://www.futurebook.net/content/direct-consumer-%E2%80%93-it%E2%80%99s-way-go> [Accessed July and August 2011]

Shatzkin, M., September 6, 2010. Publishers, Brands, and the Change to B2C. *The Shatzkin Files*. [Blog] Available at <http://www.idealog.com/blog/publishers-brands-and-the-change-to-b2c> [Accessed July 14, 2011].

Shatzkin, M., June 26, 2011a. Would million e-book-selling author John Locke be better off with a publisher? I think he very well might. *The Shatzkin Files*. [Blog] Available at <http://www.idealog.com/blog/would-million-e-book-selling-author-john-locke-be-better-off-with-a-publisher-i-think-he-very-well-might> [Accessed July 14, 2011].

Shatzkin, M., September 5, 2011b. What smaller publishers, agents, and authors need to know about e-book publishing. *The Shatzkin Files*. [Blog] Available at <http://www.idealog.com/blog/what-smaller-publishers-agents-and-authors-need-to-know-about-e-book-publishing> [Accessed September 2011].

Shuen, A., 2008. *Web 2.0: A Strategy Guide*. Sebastopol: O'Reilly Media.

SNCR: Society for New Communications Research, 2011. *Case Study: Dell uses Social Media in China Market*. [Online] Available at <http://www.marketingpower.com/ResourceLibrary/Documents/Content%20Partner%20Documents/SNCR/2011/dell_microblogging_case%20study.pdf> [Accessed July 22, 2011].

Solomon, M., Marshall, G., and Stuart, E., 2006. *Real People, Real Choices*. Upper Saddle River: Pearson Education.

Thompson, J. 2005. *Books in the Digital Age*. Cambridge: Polity Press.

Twitter, 2011. *Twitter/ Home*. [Online] Available at: <http://www.twitter.com/> [Accessed July and August 2011].

Twitter Help, 2011. *Twitter Help Center*. [Online] Available at: <https://support.twitter.com/articles/68916-following-rules-and-best-practices> [Accessed July and August 2011].

Woll, T., 2006. *Publishing for Profit*. Chicago: Chicago Review Press.

Zarrella, D. and Zarrella, A., 2011. *The Facebook Marketing Book*. Sebastopol: O'Reilly Media.

About the author:

After her first degree in computer sciences, Kim Maya Sutton held various positions in different industries, and thus, she acquired broad practical knowledge. She has furthered her academic education with a Bachelor in International Management and completed a Master of Arts in Publishing in Cambridge. During her time in Cambridge, she started teaching various undergrad and postgrad management classes; today, she teaches at Jade University of Applied Sciences in Wilhelmshaven. During her studies, she co-founded an independent publishing house and researched new marketing possibilities and customer loyalty schemes arising through the Internet.